SACRED LEGACY

SACRED LEGACY

ANCIENT WRITINGS FROM NINE WOMEN OF STRENGTH AND HONOR

MYRNA GRANT

Baker Books

A Division of Baker Book House Co
Grand Rapids, Michigan 49516

© 2003 by Myrna Grant

Published by Baker Books
a division of Baker Book House Company
P.O. Box 6287, Grand Rapids, MI 49516-6287

Printed in the United States of America

Library of Congress Cataloging-in-Publication Data
Sacred legacy : ancient writings from nine women of strength and honor / [edited by] Myrna Grant.
     p.   cm.
Includes bibliographical references.
ISBN 0-8010-6454-6 (pbk.)
     1. Christian women—Religious life. 2. Christian women—History—To 1500. 3. Christian women saints—History—To 1500. I. Grant, Myrna.
BV4527.S22 2003
270′.092′2—dc21   2003009299

For Jen

CONTENTS

PREFACE

Christian women down through the centuries have been inspired by the biblical stories of other believing women. Young Miriam, in the Moses story, innocently offered to find a nurse for the little baby in the bulrushes. Deborah, the mighty prophetess, put heart into the timid Barak and marched with ten thousand soldiers into victorious battle. The sacrificial devotion of Ruth, the blazing courage of Esther, the clever foresight of Rahab. And always there is Mary, the mother of Jesus, the prototype for all believers of trust and faith and obedience. Often in the biblical narratives, we hear the voices of these women. The grown-up Miriam sang, and so did Deborah. We have Esther's famous words, "If I perish, I perish!" We can follow Rahab's argument as she pleads persuasively for the safety of herself and her family. We know what Mary said to Gabriel.

After that, there is mostly silence. In the early church and through the premodern centuries of Christian history, monks and scholars sometimes wrote about heroic women martyrs; healers; desert mothers, who chose lives of solitude and contemplation; and reformers. We owe these writers gratitude for giving us glimpses of remarkable women whose faith and costly discipleship have thrilled and inspired both women and men throughout the ages. But what if we could hear women of the distant past tell of their own spiritual experiences? What if they could speak in their own words about their fears, struggles, disappointments, joys, and above all, how their passionate love of Jesus captivated and motivated them? The fact is, we can, in small part. Truly, very few of the educated people in the ancient world were women. And those who were, aristocrats mostly, seldom took the time or had the interest to write manuscripts devoted to their own reflections, studies, or life events. But some did. This book is a collection of the writings of nine extraordinary Christian women writers of the distant past. Scholars agree that their individual contributions are monumental. Some of them are memorialized in the stained glass windows of beautiful cathedrals. Yet, what may catch us by surprise but spark recognition as we read their writings is their humanness. A young martyr grieves as her infant is taken from her. A nun of immense sweetness writes of her lifelong prostrating headaches. Another describes her exasperation at the condescension of male colleagues. Another, in the face of her tremendous accomplishments, practically simpers that "she is a mere woman."

Activist women of the Middle Ages were often demeaned and slandered in one way or another. The church resisted and opposed their efforts at reform and independence; perhaps they were witches or heretics. Perhaps their visions and wisdom came from the devil. And if women attracted a crowd of followers, they were obviously dangerous. But spiritually gifted women persevered, faithful to the gifts and callings God had given them and to their own powerful love of Jesus. The women in this book left behind them far more than their Christian witness recorded by others. They left their own writings, which, as testament to their

10

stature, the church carefully preserved. As we read their writings, these women draw near. We hear their voices and listen with growing admiration as they record their struggles, their joyous spiritual experiences, their times of despair, their dreams, visions, and triumphs.

In the beginning of this new century, it is both tremendously humbling and encouraging for us to hear these amazing women speak. Writing on parchment with stiff pens and ink made from lampblack, they painstakingly recorded their own histories and times. Their motivation for writing, however, was far from autobiographical. They burned with zeal to preserve what the Lord himself showed them, as well as his acts in their lives. The writer of the Book of Hebrews, recounting the great heroes of the Christian faith, in describing their great feats and sufferings, observes that "the world was not worthy of them" (Heb. 11:38 NIV). The writer then ends with a startling application. "These were all commended for their faith, yet none of them received what they had been promised. God had planned something better for us so that *only together with us* would they be made perfect" (Heb. 11:39–40 NIV).

We women of today, joined together with them? It is an inspiring vision.

PERPETUA

NEW MOTHER AND MARTYR

Carthage, North Africa; 181–203

Some years ago, during the Cold War with the Soviet Union, I interviewed a self-proclaimed nun in Vilnius, Lithuania (Catholic religious orders were forbidden at that time). The woman, Niole Sudanite, had been sentenced by the Soviet authorities to an agonizing term of imprisonment in a Siberian labor camp. She had survived her sentence and was presently in Vilnius. The Lithuanian church felt Niole was a true hero of the faith and wanted a non-Lithuanian writer to interview her. Her arrest had taken place some six years before when she had been discovered helping to publish the names, trials, and whereabouts of Christians and dissidents serving sentences in the deadly labor camps of the Gulag.

Newly released, and to the frustration of the authorities, she continued her work. To avoid a second arrest as long as possible, she was "underground." To reach her, one had to pass through a chain of contacts so organized that none of the individual links knew anything other than their one assigned task. The process began as I sat in my hotel room in Vilnius, listening for a knock on the door. I had been given a Lithuanian-American translator, but after the first day of waiting in the hotel, she had become frightened by the suddenly real cloak-and-dagger aspect to her translation job and had left to join a tour group of Americans visiting the Soviet Baltic states.

After two days of nibbling on my store of nuts, crackers, and raisins, and drinking dubious-looking tap water, the knock came. Mutely I followed an unsmiling woman out of the hotel into the hilly streets of Vilnius, walking at what seemed to me a breakneck pace, turning and doubling back until I was hopelessly lost. Eventually we came to a magnificent Orthodox church. I glanced up at its beautiful domes for a second, and as my gaze returned to the street, I discovered my contact had disappeared. I walked slowly around the outside of the church, and then I stood inside, trying to pray. As I strolled around the vast interior, admiring the architecture and the candle flames wavering in front of glittering icons, I remained alert to every footstep, each cough, any movement. In the cemetery outside, I studied the iron-fenced ancient gravestones. A long time passed before I felt a light touch on my arm and a man began a fast walk quite far ahead of me. I strained to keep him in view. After passing through the city center, we approached a small park. As intent as I was not to lose him, he vanished into the crowd. I hesitated. People on the street pushed past me, irritated that I was impeding the stolid mass of ongoing pedestrians. I allowed myself to be carried along by the crowds, my apprehension growing. Ahead of me in the park I saw an empty bench. Praying I was making the right guess, I crossed into the park and sat down on the bench, pulled a small book out of my pocket, and tried to read. Suddenly a woman stood facing me. From photographs I had seen, I recognized the one I had come to interview. She was smiling lightheartedly. Backlit by the afternoon sun, her hair seemed to surround her face with a disconcerting corona of light. "Follow," she said in English. This last walk was a long one, across an iron bridge spanning the Neris River, crossing another bridge that stretched over wide railroad yards. Finally we came into a street of little houses, one of which she swiftly entered. When I reached the door, it was quickly opened. Two or three people were with her, offering me tea and fruit and settling us both on a broken sofa in the darkened room. The strange light that, in the park, I had taken to be the sun reflected in her hair now seemed to shine from her face and eyes. I found it hard to concentrate as she took my hand and said, smiling, in French, "Dear sister, my sister, I love you."

Vibia Perpetua was a young woman of North Africa who lived eighteen hundred years ago. As a new convert to Christianity, she was arrested in Thuburbo, near Carthage, by Roman authorities and at her trial sentenced to death. There had been martyrs before Perpetua, and thousands upon thousands have come after her up to the present time. Niole Sudanite in our own day came close to death during her starving years in hard labor camps. What is unique about Perpetua is that while in her Roman dungeon, she wrote an account of her arrest and imprisonment. Her manuscript, which the early church preserved as a martyr's relic, is one of the oldest and most descriptive accounts of Roman martyrdom in existence. It is also the earliest known Christian document written by a woman. In my imagination I can picture Perpetua having that same unearthly light around her that I saw in the blaze of sunlight that crowned Niole's head. As Perpetua and her slave Felicitas enter the arena to face the unleashed power of Rome and the wild beasts, I imagine her embracing Felicitas and saying as her farewell, "Dear sister, my sister, I love you."

Perpetua lived in Carthage in North Africa in the days of Septimus Severus Caesar who was Roman Emperor from 193 to 211. Her great city was second only to Rome in prosperity and administrative importance. In years to come, Carthage would develop as a major center of Christianity and learning. Several early church fathers are associated with Carthage. Tertullian, the renowned theologian of the second century who wrote that "the blood of the martyrs is the seed of the church," was living there when Perpetua was arrested, and her name appears in his writings. Saint Cyprian, who would one day become bishop of Carthage and who was later martyred, was a small child on his parents' estate near Carthage when Perpetua died. Saint Augustine, one of the greatest of church theologians, was born near Carthage and educated in its great centers of learning a century after Perpetua.

Many women of the early church appear in Scripture and manuscripts only as names, but several biographical facts are known about Perpetua. She was highborn and educated. She had two brothers, one a new convert like herself. She had a confident and lively personality. Her pregnant slave Felicitas was also a new believer. At the time of Perpetua's arrest, she was twenty or twenty-one years old, was married, and had an infant son who was nursing at her breast. Her arrest came early in the holy season of

Lent, during the time when she, among others, was being prepared for an Easter baptism.

In the midst of this process for new believers, Perpetua and Felicitas, along with three male catechumens,[1] Secundulus, Saturninus, and Revocatus, a slave, were arrested. Their offense was civil disobedience. They refused to perform a required Roman sacrifice to the pagan gods in the form of a pinch of incense in honor of the emperor.[2] Why Perpetua's small group was singled out is not known; at this time the arrests of Christians throughout the empire were sporadic. Intense empire-wide persecution of believers would begin some fifty years later during the reign of the emperor Decius.

Perpetua's father is a central actor in her diary. She begins her prison account with her father's first visit to her after her arrest. We learn from a later entry that she is his only daughter, indulged and adored by her father. He begs her to recant. She infuriates him by calmly explaining, "I cannot be called anything else than what I am, a Christian." When the time of her sentencing comes, her desperate father arrives at the public tribunal with her baby in his arms. His wild entreaties to Perpetua are so disruptive that Hilarion, the governor, has him removed and beaten with rods, a sight that greatly distresses Perpetua. The governor himself urges Perpetua to spare her own life if for no other reason than to show mercy to her distraught father and her tiny son. Seeing she is resolute, Hilarion asks Perpetua the damning question, "Are you a Christian?" This is tantamount to asking if she rebels against the authority of Rome. Perpetua answers, "I am a Christian." The others in her small group also confess Christ. All are condemned to die in the amphitheater during the upcoming festivities honoring Septimus Severus

Caesar's birthday. Perpetua writes that as the believers were led back to their dungeon cells, they rejoiced.

The Roman prison warden was not accustomed to patrician Christians among the criminal population of his jail. The prayers and singing of the believers drew him into conversations with them. In her diary, Perpetua mentions the conversion of the warden in an offhand way and records that this newly Christian official allowed Perpetua's brothers and others to join the group in the prison for meals.

The slave Felicitas was now eight months pregnant, and she and her fellow believers became greatly distressed because Roman law forbade the execution of a pregnant woman. The emperor's birthday was imminent. Still pregnant, Felicitas would be left behind when Perpetua and the others were sent into the arena. Felicitas's sentence would be carried out later and she would die in the arena with criminals who were sentenced to a public death. The Christians began to pray that her infant would be born early. As they prayed, Felicitas's labor pains began and she was delivered of a girl, whom she gave to her sister.

Perpetua's diary stops at this point. There are two addendums to the manuscript. One is written by Saturninus, who records a vision he had of the martyrs' arrival in heaven. The second addition describes the martyrdoms. Scholars believe the account was written by one of the two deacons, Tertius and Pomponius, who witnessed the executions.

On the day of Caesar's birthday, the deacon records, the prisoners were marched through Carthage from the prison to the amphitheater. Perpetua sang hymns of victory as she walked, and the men shouted warnings to the people lined along the streets and to the huge crowds in the amphitheater. The men's assertive attitude so enraged the waiting spectators in the arena that they shouted demands that the men be whipped before being given to the beasts. This was done. For a macabre joke, and to mock the two women, a mad cow was let into the arena, along with the wild beasts. After the believers were mauled by the beasts, they were dragged before the crowds to waiting gladiators who cut their throats. Perpetua's last act was to guide the hand of the gladiator to her throat.

The Acts of Perpetua and Felicitas

While I was still with the police authorities, my father out of love for me tried to dissuade me from my resolution. "Father," I said, "do you see here, for example this vase, or pitcher, or whatever it is?" "I see it," he said. "Can it be named anything else than what it really is?" I asked and he said, "No." "So I cannot be called anything else than what I am, a Christian." Enraged by my words my father came at me as though to tear out my eyes. He only annoyed me, but he left, overpowered by his diabolical arguments.

For a few days my father stayed away. I thanked the Lord and felt relieved because of my father's absence. At this time we were baptized and the Spirit instructed me not to request anything . . . except endurance of physical suffering.

A few days later we were imprisoned. I was terrified because never before had I experienced such darkness. What a terrible day! Because of crowded conditions and rough treatment by the soldiers, the heat was unbearable. My condition was aggravated by my anxiety for my baby. Then Tertius and Pomponius, those kind deacons who were taking care of our needs, paid for us to be moved for a few hours to a better part of the prison where we might refresh ourselves. Leaving the dungeon, we all went about our business. I nursed my child who was already weak from hunger. In my anxiety for the infant I spoke to my mother about him, tried to console my brother and asked that they care for my son. I suffered intensely because I sensed their agony on my account. These were the trials I had to endure for many days. Then I was granted the privilege of having my son remain with me in prison. Being relieved of my anxiety and concern for the infant, I immediately regained my strength. Suddenly the prison became my palace, and I loved being there rather than any other place. . . .[3]

A few days later there was a rumor that our case was to be heard. My father, completely exhausted from his anxiety, came from the city to see me with the intention of weakening my faith. "Daughter," he said, "have pity on my grey head. Have pity on your father if I have the honor to be called father by you. If with these hands I have brought you to the prime of your life, and if I have always favored you above your brothers, do not abandon me to the reproach of men. Consider your brothers; consider your mother and your aunt; consider your son who cannot live without you. Give up your stubbornness before you destroy all of us. None of us will be able to speak freely if anything happens to you."

These were the things my father said out of love, kissing my hands and throwing himself at my feet. With tears he called me not daughter, but woman. I was very upset because of my father's condition. He was the only member of my family who would find no reason for joy in my suffering. I tried to comfort him saying, "Whatever God wants at this tribunal will happen, for remember that our power comes not from ourselves but from God." But utterly dejected, my father left me.

One day as we were eating, we were suddenly rushed off for a hearing. We arrived at the forum and the news spread quickly throughout the area near the forum. And a huge crowd gathered. We climbed up to the prisoners' platform. All the others confessed when they were questioned. When my turn came, my father appeared with my son. Dragging me from the step, he begged: "Have pity on your son!"

Hilarion, the governor who assumed power after the death of proconsul Mimucius Timinianus, said, "Have pity on your father's grey head; have pity on your infant son; offer sacrifice for the emperor's welfare." But I answered, "I will not." Hilarion asked, "Are you a Christian?" And I answered, "I am a Christian." And when my father persisted in his attempts to dissuade me, Hilarion ordered him thrown out, and he was beaten with a rod. My father's injury hurt me as much as if I myself had been beaten. And I grieved because of his pathetic old age. Then the sentence was passed; all of us were condemned to the beasts. We were overjoyed as we went back to the prison cell. Since I was still nursing my child who was ordinarily in the cell with me, I quickly sent the deacon Pomponius to my father's house to ask for the baby, but my father refused to give him up. Then God saw to it that my child no longer needed my nursing, nor were my breasts inflamed. After that I was no longer tortured by anxiety about my child or by pain in my breasts. . . . A few days passed. Pudens, the official in charge of the prison (the official who had gradually come to admire us for our persistence), admitted many prisoners to our cell so that we might mutually encourage one another. As the day of the games drew near, my father, overwhelmed with grief, came again to see me. He began to pluck out his beard and throw it on the ground. Falling on his face before me, he cursed his old age, repeating such things as would move all creation. And I grieved because of his old age.[4]

[Perpetua then records in detail visions of victory that she and Saturus experienced in their cells. Her writing breaks off at this point and the narrative is continued by the eyewitness of the martyrdoms.]

As for Felicitas, she too was touched by God's grace in the following manner. She was pregnant when arrested, and was now in her eighth month. As the day of the contest approached she became very distressed that her martyrdom might be delayed, since the law forbade the execution of a pregnant woman. Then she later would have to shed her holy and innocent blood among common criminals. Her friends in martyrdom were equally sad at the thought of abandoning such a good friend to travel alone the same road to hope.

And so, two days before the contest, united in grief they prayed to the Lord. Immediately after the prayers her labor pains began. Because of the additional pain natural for an eighth-month delivery, she suffered greatly during the birth, and one of the prison guards taunted her; "If you're complaining now, what will you do when you'll be thrown to the wild beasts?" She answered, "Now it is I who suffer, but then another shall be in me to bear the pain for me, since I am now suffering for him." And she gave birth to a girl whom one of her sisters reared as her own daughter.

. . . We are adding an instance of Perpetua's perseverance and lively spirit. At one time the prisoners were being treated with unusual severity by the commanding officer because certain deceitful men intimated to him that the prisoners might escape by some magic spells. Perpetua openly challenged him:

"Why don't you at least allow us to freshen up, the most noble of the condemned, since we belong to Caesar and are about to fight on his birthday? Or isn't it to your credit that we should appear in good condition on that day?" The officer grimaced and blushed, then ordered that they be treated more humanely and that her brothers and others be allowed to visit and dine with them. By this time the prison warden was himself a believer.

On the day before the public games, as they were eating the last meal commonly called the free meal, they tried as much as possible to make it instead an agape.[5] In the same way they were exhorting the people, warning them to remember the judgment of God, asking them to be witnesses to the prisoners' joy in suffering and ridiculing the curiosity of the crowd. . . . Then they all left the prison amazed, and many of them began to believe.

The day of their victory dawned, and with joyful countenances they marched from the prison to the arena as though on their way to heaven. If there was any trembling, it was from joy, not fear. Perpetua followed with a quick step as a true spouse of Christ, the darling of God, her brightly flashing eyes quelling the gaze of the crowd. Felicitas too, joyful because she had safely survived childbirth and was now able to participate in the contest with the wild animals, passed from one shedding of blood to another; from midwife to gladiator. . . . As they were led through the gate they were ordered to put on different clothes; the men, those of priests of Saturn, the women, those of the priestesses of Ceres. But that noble woman stubbornly resisted to the end. She said, "We've come this far voluntarily in order to protect our rights, and we've pledged our lives not to

23

recapitulate on any such matter as this. We made this agreement with you." Injustice bowed to justice and the guard conceded that they could enter the arena in their ordinary dress. Perpetua was singing victory psalms. Revocatus, Saturninus and Saturus were warning the spectators, and as they came in sight of Hilarion they informed him by nods and gestures, "You condemn us; God will condemn you." This so infuriated the crowds that they demanded a whipping of these men in front of the line of gladiators. But the ones so punished rejoiced in that they had obtained yet another share in the Lord's suffering.

. . . at the outset of the show [Saturus] was matched against a leopard but then called back; then he was mauled by a bear on the exhibition platform. . . . When he was tied to a wild boar the professional gladiator who had tied the two together was pierced instead and died shortly after the games had ended, while Saturus was merely dragged about. And when he was tied up on the bridge in front of the bear, the bear refused to come out of his den; and so a second time Saturus was called back unharmed. [His throat was subsequently cut.]

For the young women, the devil had readied a mad cow, an animal not usually used at these games, but selected so that the women's sex would be matched with that of the animal. After being stripped and enmeshed in nets, the women were led into the arena. How horrified the people were as they saw that one was a young girl and the other, her breasts dripping with milk, had just recently given birth to a child. Consequently, both were recalled and dressed in loosely fitting gowns.

Perpetua was tossed first and fell on her back. She sat up, being more concerned with her sense of modesty than with her pain, covered her thighs with her gown

24

which had been torn down one side. Then finding her
hair clip which had fallen out, she pinned back her loose
hair thinking it not proper for a martyr to suffer with
disheveled hair; it might seem that she was mourning in
her hour of triumph. Then she stood up. Noticing that
Felicitas was badly bruised, she went to her, reached out
her hands and helped her to her feet. As they stood there
the cruelty of the crowds seem to be appeased and they
were sent to the Sanavivarian Gate.[6] There Perpetua was
taken care of by a certain [Christian teacher], Rusticus,
who stayed near her. She seemed to be waking from a
deep sleep (so completely had she been entranced and
imbued by the Spirit). She began to look around her
and to everyone's astonishment asked, "When are we
going to be led out to that cow, or whatever it is?" She
would not believe that it had already happened until
she saw the various markings of the tossing on her body
and clothing. Then calling for her brother she said to
him and the [teacher], "Remain strong in your faith and
love one another. Do not let our excruciating suffering
become a stumbling block for you."[7]

. . . And when the crowd demanded that the prisoners
be brought out into the open so that they might feast
their eyes on death by the sword, they voluntarily arose
and moved where the crowd wanted them. Before doing
so they kissed each other so that their martyrdom would
be completely perfected by the rite of the kiss of peace.

. . . Perpetua . . . groaning as she was struck between
the ribs, took the gladiator's trembling hand and guided
it to her throat. Perhaps it was that so great a woman . . .
could not have been slain had she not herself willed it.[8]

2

EGERIA

PILGRIM HISTORIAN

Spain or France, Pilgrimage of 381–384

When my son Andrew was seven years old, I took him and his three siblings along on a working trip to Africa. In the journal that he kept, his first entry, written on the plane in the laborious cursive of childhood reads, "When I started to Africa, I was scared."

Not only seven-year-olds are apprehensive at the beginning of a distant journey. Even with transportation that would have astonished the ancients, first-time sight-seers of today still have a mixed sense both of adventure and trepidation on embarking on travel to foreign lands. Yet flying high above ocean storms, treacherous mountains, burning deserts, and local wars, they escape many of the ordeals and perils of travel in antiquity.

In the first century, the intrepid apostle Paul gave a dramatic picture of his own arduous journeys throughout the Roman Empire. "Three times I was shipwrecked. . . . I have traveled many weary miles, I have faced danger from flooded rivers and from robbers . . . in the deserts and in the stormy seas. . . . I have lived with weariness and pain and sleepless nights. Often I have been hungry and thirsty and have gone without food . . . without enough clothing to keep me warm" (2 Cor. 11:26–27).

What drove the apostle was his selfless evangelistic fervor to bring salvation to the gentile world. But soon enough after Paul, early Christians in Europe began their own journeys east to famous biblical sites or to shrines of Christian martyrs. Their motivations to seek out holy places were personal and spiritual, grounded in an impulse originating from the dawn of time. From the beginning of human history, early peoples built barrows, erected great stones, or set apart caves as sacred sites. In pagan antiquity and into the Roman-Christian era, hallowed places associated with heroes, gods, or oracles were venerated. Devotees who wanted to petition or worship a spirit or god would undertake a journey to the place associated with the divinity. In the early church, believers deeply reverenced the distant villages where Jesus was born and carried out his ministry. Most sacred to them was Jerusalem, city of his death and resurrection. The pious longed to see these Christian sites and the Old Testament geographical landmarks named in Scripture. Mount Sinai, where the Ten Commandments were given; the Red Sea, where the Egyptians perished; and Nebo, the mountain from which Moses saw the Promised Land, were honored sites in biblical history. From as early as the second century, Christians came to reverence holy objects connected to the lives of saints and martyrs and to Christ himself, such as the holy nails, the holy lance, and the holy coat, venerated as relics of Christ's passion.

By the fourth century, after the dramatic conversion of Emperor Constantine in 312, Christianity was declared the official religion of the Roman Empire. Constantine initiated a widespread campaign to build churches, cathedrals, and basilicas. He gave vast land holdings and other lavish gifts to the church and made Byzantium his capital city, renaming it Constantinople.

The site of Christ's tomb in Jerusalem had been discovered, and Constantine ordered a great church to be built over this "holy of holies where Christ had been laid to rest."[1] Over the grave of Saint Peter in Rome he built a basilica, timber-roofed, following the model of the Roman civic hall. Throughout the Empire, he transformed many existing Roman basilicas into Christian cathedrals, some to house the bones and relics of heroic martyrs. Even the most sacred relic of all, the true cross, had been found in Jerusalem by Constantine's mother, Helena, who had been sent to the Holy City to oversee Constantine's building programs.

These sacred discoveries and the exciting construction of great Christian edifices throughout Constantine's empire were tremendously energizing to believers and ushered in a great age of pilgrimage that continued through the Middle Ages as people set out to see the holy wonders for themselves. Constantine encouraged the act of pilgrimage,[2] viewing journeys of the pious as means to deepen the devotion of believers and strengthen the church. Pilgrims hoped to receive special blessings at the shrines and holy places they visited, to experience the miraculous, and to increase their understanding of Scripture.

Egeria was such a pilgrim, yet two remarkable things distinguish Egeria. One was her unusual courage. She traveled east as a woman, alone in the particularly unsettled time of the late fourth century in Europe. The western half of the Roman Empire in which she lived had begun to fragment into smaller and smaller kingdoms. The powerful unity of the once invincible empire was crumbling, its great western cities crushed by invading Germanic Visigoths from the North. Historic Athens and mighty Rome had already fallen to the barbarian king, Alaric I. The western emperors had long since fled Rome for Ravenna in the Italian north. The diminished Caesar of Egeria's day was reputed to say that he knew nothing of Rome beyond the fact that it was the name of his pet chicken.[3]

In addition to civil unrest and unforeseeable misadventures, Egeria had to contend with the scorching heat, soaking rains, storms at sea, and fear of losing her way that were so much a part of the apostle Paul's missionary journeys.

Egeria's second achievement was that she wrote a remarkable diary. The travel records of her time were little more than tedious lists of destinations. Egeria wrote in rich detail describing the places, customs, conversations, and people she encountered. She wrote nothing of the difficulties she must have encountered or the fears she might have had. In reading her travelogue, we find nothing about why she started out, and as she makes her way across vast land areas, she appears intrepid. Unlike my small son, Andrew, on his way to the immensities of Africa, there is little likelihood that Egeria would have begun the lost first pages of her diary with "When I started out, I was afraid."

Scholars are intrigued by Egeria because so little is known about her. She was born late in the fourth century, possibly in Spain. She is thought to have been a nun because ancient writers who read her journal called her "blessed and holy" and an abbess.[4] Evidenced by her writings, she was an educated woman with unusual knowledge of Scripture, and she apparently had wide contacts in monastic and influential circles. She seems to have been well received and respected by the priests, hermits, and monks she met throughout her travels. She may have been a person of high rank before entering the convent, so that the officials she encountered along the way would have given her military escorts and other help to ease her way.[5] She was likely to have been wealthy, able to undertake such arduous travel because she had friends, servants, goods, and comforts to accompany her. Of any such advantages she writes nothing.

Before she ended her pilgrimage, Egeria had traveled to the fabled eastern cities of Constantine's new Constantinople and to old Alexandria. She visited the great Roman city of Antioch where the apostles Paul and Peter had preached the gospel. She made her way across barren wilderness to reach isolated desert monasteries. In Palestine she retraced the footsteps of Jesus from Bethlehem and Nazareth to the Sea of Galilee. She lingered long in the (Roman) backwater city of Jerusalem where she wrote of the sites, buildings, and liturgy of the Christian church there.

A remarkable letter in praise of Egeria was written by the seventh-century monk Valerius. Of her he wrote:

A longing for God's grace set on fire this most blessed nun Egeria. In the strength of the glorious Lord she fearlessly set out on an immense journey to the other side of the world. Guided by God, she pressed on until after a time she reached what she longed for, the most holy places of the birth, passion and resurrection of the Lord. . . . First with great industry, she perused all the books of the Old and New Testaments, and discovered all their descriptions of the holy deserts. Then in eager haste (though it was to take many years) she set out, with God's help to explore them.[6]

We cannot but blush at this woman, dearest brothers—we in the full enjoyment of our bodily health and strength. Embracing the example of the holy Patriarch Abraham, she transformed the weakness of her sex into an iron strength, that she might win the reward of eternal life; and while, compassed about with her weakness, she trod this earth, she was obtaining paradise in calm and exultant glory. Though a native of Ocean's western shore, she became familiar with the East . . . here she refused rest . . . here she inflicted material burdens on her earthly body . . . here, by her own will and choice she accepted the labors of pilgrimage, that she might . . . inherit a heavenly kingdom.[7]

Egeria's Diary

The surviving manuscript begins with the end of a sentence.

. . . were shown according to the Scriptures. As we moved along, we came to a certain place where the mountains through which we were traveling, opened out to form an immense valley, vast, quite flat and extremely beautiful, and across the valley there appeared Sinai, God's holy mountain. This place where the mountains opened adjoins the spot where the Graves of Lust are located . . . [see Num. 11:34].[8] When one reaches this place, "It is customary," said the holy men who were guiding us and so advised us, "for those who are coming to say a prayer when, for the first time and from this place, the mountain of God comes into view." And that is what we did.[9]

. . . Then I remembered that it was written that Saint John [the Baptist] had baptized in Ennon near Salim [see John 3:23], I asked of [the priest] how far away that place was. Whereupon the saintly priest said, "It is two hundred feet from here. If you wish, I can lead you there on foot right away. The large amount of pure water, which you see in this village, comes from this very spring." I then thanked him and asked him to guide us to that place; and he did so. We went all the way on foot across a very pleasant valley with him until we came to a very beautiful fruit orchard in the center of which he showed us a spring of the very purest and best water which at once gives rise to a real stream. In front of the spring there is a sort of pool where it seems that Saint John the Baptist administered baptism. . . . After we had received from the priest's gifts out of the orchard of Saint John the Baptist, and also from the holy monks whose cells are in the same orchard, we continued on the way we were going, continually giving thanks to God. And so, we traveled for some time through the valley of the Jordan on the bank above this river, for our route lay along this way for some distance. Suddenly we saw the city of the holy prophet Elias [Elijah], namely Thesbe [Tishbe in Gilead] from which he took the name, Elias the Thesbite. Even today the cave is there where the holy man sat and there too is the tomb of the holy man Jepthah, whose name we read in the books of the Judges [see Judg. 11:1; 12:1–7]. And giving thanks there to God in accord with our custom we continued on our journey.[10]

The following passage is invaluable as one of the few surviving contemporary descriptions of early church customs in Jerusalem.

I must also describe how those who are baptized at Easter are instructed. Whoever gives his name does so the day before Lent and the priest notes down all their names and this is before those eight weeks during which as I have said Lent is observed here. When the priest has noted down everyone's name, then on the following day, the first day of Lent, on which the eight weeks begin, a throne is set up for the bishop in the center of the major church, the Martyrium.[11] The priests sit on stools on both sides and all the clergy stand around. One by one the candidates are led forward in such a way that the men come with their godfathers and the women with their godmothers.

Then the bishop questions individually the neighbors of this one who has come up, inquiring, "Does he live a good life? Does he obey his parents? Is he a drunkard or a liar?" And he seeks out in the man other vices which are more serious. If the person proves to be guiltless in all these matters concerning which the bishop has questioned the witnesses who are present, he notes down the man's name in his own hand. If however he is accused of anything, the bishop orders him to go out and says, "Let him amend his life and when he has done so, let him then approach the baptismal font." He makes the same inquiry of both men and women. If however, someone is a stranger, he cannot easily receive baptism, unless he has witnesses who know him.

Ladies, my sisters, I must describe this, lest you think that it is done without explanation. It is the custom here, throughout the forty days of which there is fasting, for those who are preparing for baptism to be exorcized by the clergy early in the morning as soon as the dismissal from the morning service has been given. . . . Immediately a throne is placed for the bishop in the major church, the Martyrium. All those who are to be baptized, both men and women, sit closely around the bishop, while the godfathers and godmothers stand there; and indeed all of the people who wish to listen may enter and sit down, provided they are of the faithful. A catechumen[12] however may not enter at the time when the bishop is teaching the law. He does so in this way: beginning with Genesis he goes through all of Scripture in those forty days, expounding first its literal meaning and then explaining the spiritual meaning. In the course of these days everything is taught, not only the Resurrection, but concerning the body of faith. . . . When five weeks of instruction have been completed, they then receive the Creed. He explains the meaning of each of the phrases of the Creed in the same way he explained the Holy Scripture, expounding first the literal and then the spiritual sense. In this fashion, the Creed is taught. . . . And thus they are taught for three hours[13] a day for seven weeks. . . . Now when seven weeks have gone by and there remains only Holy Week, which is here called the Great Week[14] then the bishop comes in the morning to the major church, the Martyrium. To the rear, at the apse[15] behind the altar, a throne is placed for the bishop, and one by one they come forth, the men with their godfathers, the women with their godmothers. And each one recites the Creed back to the bishop. After the Creed has been recited back to the bishop, he delivers a homily to them all. . . .[16]

3

DHUODA

ROYAL PRISONER

Frankish Kingdom, 803–843

I have only one photograph of my mother. She is young and beautiful, smiling shyly, wrapped in a polka-dotted cotton robe and standing on the veranda of the tuberculosis sanitarium where she eventually died. She was diagnosed when she was twenty-four years old with two small children, myself, age two, and my brother, age seven. Tuberculosis, one of the oldest diseases of humankind, used to be called "consumption" or the "white plague," but we called it "TB." Diagnosed with tuberculosis, patients were immediately quarantined in sanitariums where months, often years, of bed rest, fresh air, and in extreme cases, surgeries, were the only recourse. Medications to treat the disease were introduced in the mid-twentieth century, but too late to save my mother. Because of the highly infectious nature of the disease, visitors were not allowed. Sometimes my brother and I were taken to the steep lawns of the sanitarium to allow my mother to glimpse us from a high veranda. I still have a photograph of myself, my five-year-old face screwed up against the glare of the sun, in coat, wide-brimmed hat, white gloves, and shiny shoes trying to see my mother, who, I was told, was waving to me. My mother's courage was great. In spite of an increasingly hopeless diagnosis and with no religious faith to sustain her, she presented a public persona of humorous optimism. Now that I am a mother, I can imagine the pain she endured in the long years of separation from her children. She died when I was ten without ever having left the sanitarium.

The Sunday after my mother died, my Anglican foster mother astonished me by taking me into the unknown territory of a Baptist church officiated by a minister called Dr. Priddle. He had been the chaplain on duty at my mother's deathbed and had officiated at her funeral. Perhaps my foster mother's venture into the world of the Baptists was energized by an obligation to thank him or give him a message. Dr. Priddle began his sermon with an anecdote. "Last week I was called to the bedside of a young woman who was dying of tuberculosis," he began. "This woman asked me, 'Dr. Priddle, is there a life after death?'"

That's all my child's mind can remember of that strange Sunday morning. I do not doubt that the good Baptist preacher led my mother to faith in Christ. This small vignette from a fleeting childhood memory has lifted my heart countless times as I think of my mother and the loss to both of us of each other.

Dhuoda was a mother who was also tragically separated from her children. I sometimes fancy that in heaven my mother has met Dhuoda, a thousand years her senior. I can picture them gently smiling at each other's stories.

Dhuoda was a noblewoman, born at the beginning of the ninth century into a time of a short-lived but brilliant cultural revival in the Frankish empire. The great Charlemagne was still emperor of his vast kingdom that extended across Western and Central Europe. His court in Aachen in north central Germany was a lively Christian center of learning and the arts. Dhuoda was taught Latin and Greek, and studied Scripture, theology, and the books of the doctors of the church. When Dhuoda was eleven years old, Charlemagne died, and his empire along with him. At the appropriate time, and according to the aristocratic custom of arranging marriages for political advantage, Dhuoda's parents betrothed her to Bernard, a military noble of great renown, who was a second cousin to Charlemagne. She and Bernard were married in 823, when Dhuoda was twenty. Her wedding was spectacular, taking place in the imperial cathedral at Aachen, attended by the entire royal court and by the emperor Louis I. Called Louis the Pious, he was Bernard's godfather and Charlemagne's heir and only son, who ruled until his death in 840.

In 826 a son, William, was born to Dhuoda and Bernard. Now that Bernard had sired an heir, Louis immediately appointed him commander of the emperor's campaign against distant Spain, a land bordering the southernmost extreme of the empire. Dhuoda was sent away from court to set up her household in one of Bernard's castles in the town of Uzes in Septimania. Eventually Bernard returned from Spain, and Louis appointed him royal chamberlain, a post second in authority only to the emperor, requiring him to live at court. Dhuoda remained in her own household with her son William.

In 840 King Louis died, and great dissent arose among his heirs, who warred against each other for the crown. At first Bernard prudently withdrew to summer with Dhuoda in Uzes. The following spring, their second son was born. Bernard then decided to join forces fighting against Louis's youngest son, Charles, and left for the campaign against him. Catastrophically, Bernard chose the losing side and Charles's forces prevailed. In an effort to escape the charge of treason and to reconcile with the new emperor, Bernard sent their now fourteen-year-old son, William, from Septimania to Charles's court at Aachen as proof of his new loyalty. Bernard waited in Aquitaine in the south, and sent for his infant son, yet unnamed and unbaptized, to be taken from Dhuoda and brought to him by the bishop of Aquitaine.

Despite her loneliness and the loss of both her sons, Dhuoda had experience and sophistication enough to picture only too well the danger young William was in at court as the son of a famous traitor. Plots, betrayals, and intrigues would swirl around him. Attempts would be made to defame him before the emperor. What she wrote to him would have had to be discreet; she decided to send him counsel in the form of a manual on how to live a faithful Christian life at court.

She finished writing the manual in the year of her untimely death in 843. Her book was duly delivered to William. But tragically, Dhuoda's family was not destined to outlive her for long. In 843 the Treaty of Verdun divided the warring empire among Louis's three surviving sons, and brutal retribution of rebel nobles followed. In 844 Bernard was arrested and executed for treason. Young William fled the court and joined rebels against the emperor who had killed his father. William, too, was captured and executed. The fate of Dhuoda's unnamed infant is unknown. In the end, nothing was left of the family line, its honor, its wealth, and its great estates but Dhuoda's small book for her son William.

The Handbook for William

The Manual Begins

Having noticed that most women in this world are able to live with and enjoy their children, but seeing myself, Dhuoda, living far from you, my dear son William, filled with anxiety because of this, and with the desire to be of aid to you, I am sending you this little book written by me for your scrutiny and education, rejoicing in the fact that, though I am absent in body, this little book will recall to your mind, as you read it, the things you are required to do for my sake.[1]

The Prologue

Dhuoda, although fragile in sense, living unworthily among worthy women, nevertheless your mother, William, to you now is my manual's word addressed.
. . . I hope that, busy as you are with mundane and secular preoccupations you will not neglect frequently to read in this little book sent by me to you, for the sake of my memory, as if you were looking in a mirror or at a chessboard. Even if you increase your possessions of books, may it please you to read frequently this my little work, and you will be able to understand useful things with the aid of God. You will find in it all you desire to know, set down briefly; you will also find a mirror in which you undoubtedly will be able to see the salvation of your soul.[2]

On God

I am thinking now of those whose stories I have heard read and also of some of my relatives, and yours, also,

41

whom I have known; they were powerful in this world and are no more. Perhaps they are with God because of their merits, but they are not present in body on earth. For them and for others I pray on bended knee: *Requiem aeternam*. When I consider these things and that death is to come, I fear the things to come. Therefore He is to be feared, loved and certainly to be believed to be immortal Who without diminution is Ever-Powerful King, commanding and performing whatever He wishes. All things are placed in His will and His power. "There is none who can resist His will saying, Why hast Thou done thus?" He Himself is the God of the universe; He is the power, the kingdom and the empire. Concerning His power, the most blessed Daniel firmly said, "His power is an everlasting power that shall not be taken away: and His kingdom shall not be destroyed."[3]

Moral Lesson

And what shall I say, a fragile vessel that I am? I shall turn to others as a friend. To be sure, if the heavens and the earth were spread through the air like a parchment, and if all the various gulfs of the sea were transformed into ink, and if all the inhabitants of the earth born into this world from the beginning of humankind up to now were scribes, which is an impossible thing contrary to nature, they would not be able to comprehend (in writing) the greatness, the breadth, the height, the sublimity, the profundity of the Almighty or tell the divinity, wisdom, piety, and clemency of Him who is called God. Since He is thus and so great that no one can comprehend His essence, I beg you to fear Him and to love Him with all your heart, all your mind, all your understanding, to bless Him in all your ways and deeds and to sing, "For He is good, for His mercy endureth forever!"[4]

Admonition

I also admonish you, O my handsome and lovable son William, that amid the mundane cares of this world you not neglect the acquisition of many books in which you may understand and learn something better than is written here concerning God your Creator through the teaching of the most blessed doctors. Beseech Him, cherish Him, love Him; if you do so, He will be a Keeper, a Leader, a Companion and a Fatherland for you, the Way, the Truth and the Life, granting you generous prosperity in the world, and He will turn your enemies to peace. What more can I say? Your admonisher, Dhuoda, is always with you, son, and if I be absent because of death, which must come, you will have this little book of moral teaching as a memorial; and in it you will be able to see me as the reflection in a mirror, reading and praying to God in mind and body; and you will find fully set down the duties you must perform for me. Son, you will have other teachers who will teach you other documents of greater utility, but not under the same conditions, not with a soul burning in their breasts as I your mother have, O firstborn son.[5]

On Reverence in Prayer

Prayer is called *oratio*, "prayer" sort of *oris ratio*, "reason of the mouth." But I Dhuoda, lukewarm and lazy, weak and always tending toward that which is low, neither a long nor a short prayer pleases me. But I place my hope in Him, Who offers to His faithful the freedom to pray. And you, son William, keep watch, ask of Him and pray in a short, firm, and pure speech. Say, not only in the church, but wherever the opportunity presents itself, pray and say, "Mercy-giving and Merciful, Just and Pious, Clement and True, have pity on Your creation, whom You created and redeemed with Your blood; have pity on me, and grant that I may walk in Your paths and Your justice; give me memory and sense that I may understand, believe, love, fear, praise, and thank You and be perfect in every good work through proper faith and goodwill, O Lord my God. Amen."[6]

That You Must Be Kind to Great and Small

It is not necessary for me to tell you this, that the example of the greatest, oldest, and best leaders must be followed in dealing with inferiors, for, though far from me, you will have noticed it yourself; also do not doubt that the lesser ones may rise to the heights of offering models for prelates. Therefore, I urge you not to be slow in joining yourself to them, in greater and lesser services.

God is the shaper of the good and the bad in heaven and on earth. For the sake of His lesser ones, He deigned to reveal His presence here below, for, as the Fathers say, although He was the Supreme Creator of all, He was willing to take on the form of a slave. He raises the powerful in order to plunge them into the depths, and He exalts the humble, that they may rise to the heights. . . . And if He, great as He is, comports Himself thus toward the lesser ones, what should we, small as we are, do toward those who are worse off? Those who are able ought to help them. And according to the urgings and words of the Apostle Paul, bear one another's burdens. Love all that you may be loved by all, cherish that you may be cherished; if you love all, all will love you; if you individually, they plurally. It is written in the *Grammar* of the poet Donatus, "I loved you and am loved by you, I kiss you and am kissed by you."[7]

A Special Admonition to Correct Various Habits

To attain model behavior for a human being requires a great effort and studious labor . . . not only against the men of this world, burning with envy, must one fight, but also, as St. Paul says, against spirits of wickedness in high places. There are those who seem to flourish in the world and who are rich in possessions, but, because of some secret malice, do not cease envying and molesting others, as much as they can, and this by dissimulation. You have and will have books in which you may read, page through, ruminate on, scrutinize, and understand, or even teachers to instruct you, and these will furnish you with models to follow in the performance of both your duties. . . .[8]

On the Reconciliation of Sin

If it should happen my son, that you do something bad, or even if you feel your soul is afflicted, hasten as soon as you can to make amends in all things. Turn to Him Who sees everything; always bear witness, externally as well as internally, of your guilt and worthlessness until you have given complete satisfaction, saying, "The sins of my youth and my ignorance, do not remember. I beg you, Lord, do not destroy me with my iniquities, and do not keep my faults to the end in Thy wrath. But in accord with Thy ancient clemency, and Thy great goodness, come to my aid, for Thou art merciful."[9]

Reciting Psalms

Finally, William, my son, since Psalms possess so many and such virtues, I urge and admonish you to recite them frequently for yourself and your father, as well as for all living, and also for those who are dear to you, also for all the faithful dead and for those whose memory was consigned to you from above, including those whom you may add to the list. Also for the remedy of my soul, do not forget to recite the Psalms which you have chosen, so that when the last day of life comes for me, I will have the merit of being placed, not on the left with the sinners, but on the right with the good and faithful, and to be taken up into heaven.[10]

Finis

Have frequent recourse to this little book. Always be, noble child, strong and brave in Christ! This book was begun during the second year after the death of the former emperor, Louis, the 30th of November, Saint Andrew's Day, at the beginning of Advent. It was finished, by the aid of God, on the second of February, the Feast of the Purification of the blessed ever-virgin Mary, under the propitious reign of Christ, awaiting the king whom God will designate.

Reader, pray for Dhuoda, if you wish to have the merit of seeing Christ in eternal happiness. Here ends, thanks be to God, the Manual of William, according to the word of the Gospel, "It is finished."[11]

HILDEGARD

GENIUS REFORMER

Bingen, Germany; 1098–1179

A few years ago I was in a bookstore in Jerusalem. The owner was an acquaintance of one of my faculty colleagues in America. When he learned that I was a writer, the bookstore owner became animated. He had a relative who wrote poetry in English and who worked at the palace of the Armenian patriarch. Would I be willing to go along with him to the palace to meet the poet and hear his poetry? I was very hot and footsore but he was eager and insistent. In a matter of minutes we were making our way through the Old City on narrow streets, through a passageway that opened onto a courtyard surrounded by several levels of doors that appeared to be carved into a great stone cliff. Passing through one of these doors, we entered a dazzling corridor of gilt walls and crystal chandeliers. Sitting on a chair halfway along the resplendent hallway was the poet. With elaborate courtesy I was handed off to him and spent the next hour in a glittering anteroom dutifully listening to his English poetry. The patriarch had been told that a North American writer was in the palace visiting the poet. One of his staff politely interrupted the reading and asked if I would meet the patriarch when we were finished. I was suddenly aware that my bare feet in my sandals were grimy with Jerusalem dust. My face was salty from the heat, my hair damp. I was carrying a plastic shopping bag. Was I to meet the exalted spiritual leader of Armenians around the world in a rumpled sleeveless sundress? Yet how would one refuse? And who *were* the Armenians? Later, a guide silently led me to a modest hallway and into a dimly lit bedroom. There an elderly man in blue-and-white striped pajamas sat up in bed. Above his head I could make out an ornately framed picture of him in his ecclesiastical regalia as patriarch. Three men stood around the bed looking at me. I felt a shiver of fear. How could I get out of this place if I wanted to? How could it be right that I was in the bedroom of the patriarch? What did they want of me?

One of the men offered me a confection on a gold plate. I attempted a smiling interest. What was this delicious-looking item? It was called Turkish Delight. As a reader of *The Lion, the Witch, and the Wardrobe,* I took this to be an alarming sign. I was then offered coffee from a jumble of little cups and pots on a silver tray by the bedside. After having declined the Turkish Delight, I accepted a small cup of suspiciously thick Turkish coffee. I endeavored to make small talk and to answer the patriarch's courteous questions. When the coffee drinking was finished, the patriarch beckoned me closer to his bed. He held out his empty cup.

"It is the custom," said one of the men, "for a woman to read the coffee grounds." I wondered what he could possibly mean. Was this some kind of euphemism for what I did not know? Was this humor? The patriarch's expression was expectant. With great reluctance, I took his cup. The grounds patterned the bottom and side of the cup. The patriarch shifted slightly to hear me better. Surely it was iniquitous for me to pretend to read the coffee grounds. For a fleeting moment I thought to reproach the patriarch for indulging in fortune-telling. *The patriarch?* "Well," I said, scrutinizing the inside of his cup, "I can see that you are a man who loves God." He nodded gravely. "I can see that from your early childhood you have studied the Scriptures." Another nod. This time did he look pleased? "And you have spent your life serving God." I pondered the grounds further. "And I see that God will greatly bless you for all you have done for him." I handed the cup to one of the men.

The patriarch appeared content. He reached out his arm and placed it on my head in a long blessing. Then, to my relief, I was led through the maze of rooms and corridors out into the street. I had indeed escaped without a hair harmed, but I continued to feel uneasy. Why had I allowed myself, in an unknown city, to be intimidated into uncertain situations by strangers? The inane answer: I hadn't wanted to offend.

The formidable Hildegard of Bingen, born eight long and patriarchal centuries ago, had no such timid limitations. Throughout her lifetime she confronted the highest rulers of spiritual and temporal realms whom she judged to be in sore need of repentance. She disregarded the outrage of the everyday folk of the countryside who were scandalized at her doings. Her lavish gifts as abbess, teacher, preacher, healer, theologian, administrator, diplomat, scientist, historian, composer, poet, playwright, and writer were unfettered. To those who were confounded by her power and influence she cannily observed that since she was only a "mere woman and inadequate," she was living proof that God's strength was made perfect in weakness.

Hildegard was born in Bockelheim, Germany, at the end of the eleventh century, a cruel and schismatic time throughout Europe. In the church, divisions, heresy, and superstitions abounded. The Inquisition flourished. The Christian armies of the First Crusade, who had taken Jerusalem from Islam in July of 1099, had "purified" the Holy City by a massacre of its Muslim inhabitants. In German lands, a brutal civil war created bitter and enduring enmity between the warring factions of the pope and the emperor.

The infant Hildegard was the tenth and frailest child of a noble couple who designated her as their "tithe" to God. They would give her to the church. At the early age of three, Hildegard began to suffer from severe headaches, which were to afflict her throughout her life. Along with the pain came luminous visions of objects in the form of intense light. She kept these visions secret into her middle age. In spite of her precarious health, at the age of seven or eight, Hildegard was sent to be educated by her reclusive aunt, Jutta, a holy woman who eventually founded a Benedictine convent in Disibodenberg, near the present-day town of Mainz. Hildegard's instruction was rudimentary, but she was an eager reader and had access to books by such writers as the Roman philosopher Boethuis. She also gained an extensive knowledge of Scripture. She was fortunate in her parents' choice of a Benedictine education. The Benedictines considered study an important part of daily life and their monasteries often had fine libraries. Their communities frequently were responsible for rescuing classical knowledge that had been threatened with extinction.[1] When she was a young teen, Hildegard made her own decision to become a nun and formally joined her aunt's convent as a novice. In ensuing years, when Jutta became too aged to carry on her work as abbess, it was Hildegard who succeeded her as Mother Superior of the convent. This gave Hildegard a seat on the king's council and the rank of nobility equivalent to a temporal peer.[2] Hildegard's deep devotion to her sisters at the convent extended to inventing with them a secret language which had twenty-three letters and a glossary of nine hundred words that they used to speak privately to one another when strangers were present.[3] Later in her life, around the age of fifty, she determined that her convent would be independent of the Benedictine monks who governed them. After an intense struggle, she prevailed. In 1148 she accomplished the exceptional feat of raising the large sums of money needed and founded her own convent at Rupertsberg, near Bingen. "A monastery founded by a woman, not an emperor, bishop or prince and a successful establishment at that . . . was unprecedented, a miracle."[4]

Hildegard has been called one of the greatest intellectuals of the West.[5] Her scholarly achievements were remarkably wide-ranging. As abbess at Disibodenberg she was able to study the natural world within the orchards and gardens of the convent, and she shared deeply the great medieval love of nature.[6] Convent gardens in the spring and summer were often sanctuaries of rest and recuperation for the ill. Medicines were culled from the *herbularis*, the herb-bed whose leaves and roots were used for salves and potions, and it was the herbularis that commanded Hildegard's great interest. The sisters grew yarrow to heal wounds and prevent infections; wild beet for burns; sweet cicely for insomnia; basil for insect bites; sage, the medieval cure-all; and nutmeg, praised by Hildegard as protection from falling from high places.

Hildegard's powerfully analytic mind was challenged by the multitude of cures, antidotes, and remedial claims for plants, herbs, trees, and minerals. Her research went far beyond the practical skills of her community. She studied available medical manuscripts, conducted her own experiments, and assembled a vast body of knowledge that formed the basis for two widely circulated medical textbooks. In *Causa* she categorized the herbal properties of more than two hundred medicinal herbs, giving the German as well as Latin names of the plants, thus making them easier to identify. These works, in which she described the qualities of plants, trees, birds, and animals that could be used for remedies, were the sources of choice for doctors and healers all over Europe for over a century. She also compiled a collection of the traits and habits of animals and applied their characteristics to moral comparisons for the edification of Christians.

In the summer of 1140, the course of her life and duties as an abbess radically changed. She experienced a unique and overpowering vision that, she said, bestowed on her an immediate and full understanding of the Psalms, the Gospels, and other religious texts. She wrote, "A fiery light of exceeding brilliance came and permeated my whole brain, and inflamed my whole heart and my whole breast, not like a burning but like a warming flame, as the sun warms anything its rays touch."[7]

Moreover, she was commanded to write down everything that she would observe and be taught in future visions. Hildegard strongly resisted. Her health was poor. Her education was inadequate. She was only a "poor little figure of a woman," and there were already enough spiritual books for people to read. Her refusal to commit her revelations to writing resulted in such a serious bout of ill health that eventually she yielded, encouraged by a monk who became her lifelong secretary. Although Hildegard had no doubt about the divine origin of her visions, she was a sophisticated woman aware of the deadly reach of the Inquisition—the great danger of being branded a heretic. She sought the approval of the church for her writing, sending some of her work to the great Saint Bernard, abbot of Clairvaux, for his endorsement. His answer to her was guarded, but he dispatched her manuscript to Pope Eugenius III who, to her delight, gave her his approval and encouraged her to continue writing. The endorsement of the pope made Hildegard widely known. The book she produced was *Scivias,* completed in 1151 after ten years of labor.

In addition to *Scivias,* she wrote two other visionary works, *Liber Vitae Meritorium,* "Book of Life's Merits," 1160–63, and *Liber Divinorium Operum,* "Book of Divine Works," 1163. The three books record twenty-six visions in all. Her presentation of the visions follows a pattern: first she is confronted by a bright light that radiates over a striking tableau, such as a mountain or abyss; then this image and the surrounding figures are explained by "a voice from Heaven" in passages many times greater in length than the original image.[8] In these works she expounded her theology of humankind, which she viewed as the peak of God's creation, a mirror through which the splendor of the universe is reflected. Distinctive to her writings is her exalted view of women, a contrast to the medieval view expressed by Tertullian who said of women, "You are the devil's gateway . . . you are she who persuaded him whom, the devil did not dare attack . . . do you not know that every one of you is an Eve? The sentence of God on your sex lives on."[9]

Saint Jerome, eminent doctor of the church, warned, "Lift the corner of a [woman's] dress and you will find the tip of the [devil's] tail." In contrast, Hildegard extolled the role of women in the world. Chaste nuns shone in their primacy and brilliance before the throne of God, but all women were to be acclaimed as life-givers, links between God and his creation, their feminine principle representing wisdom, love, creative energy, synergy, and beauty.[10]

Music gave Hildegard respite from the intense focus of her writings and the discipline of the Benedictine rule of life. To her, music was the means by which humans could attain something of the bliss of lost Paradise. With no formal musical training, Hildegard began to compose devotional hymns and chant sequences for the nuns in her convent in honor of the saints and the Virgin Mary. Extremely unusual for her time, she claimed authorship for all her compositions, supervising their copying into manuscripts, which were compiled into her book *Symphonia Armonie Revelationum*. Her music has a haunting and improvisatory quality, and her melodies, written as they were for women's voices, have a wide range of octaves and many dramatic leaps.[11]

Hildegard was also a lyric poet, combining her gifts of poetry and music in writing a play called *Ordo Virtutum*, "Play of Virtues," which sets to music eighty-two original poems, a work that is thought to have been performed in her own convent and is one of the earliest known examples of a morality play. To clarify her visions for others, she produced a magnificent series of illustrations and manuscript illuminations.

Hildegard's mystical and theological writings were protected from criticism, but her life was not. People were scandalized that she had a public ministry of preaching and counseling and that she traveled around the country giving instruction and warnings to men in high authority. Such goings-on were unheard of for a nun. Opponents called her a frenzied prophetess, an eccentric, and, most serious of all, a demon-possessed woman. She was accused of insolence and pride for claiming that she was divinely inspired and for roundly criticizing the bitter and open conflict between church and secular rulers. She did not hesitate to use her family's worldly connections among the aristocracy to gain access to offending high church and royal officials. When distance prevented her from addressing dignitaries in person, she wrote impassioned letters of entreaty and condemnation to successive popes, bishops, and emperors. These struggles with church authorities continued throughout her long life. Even in her last year of life, when she was a venerable eighty, she had a rancorous dispute with the church hierarchy. The conflict concerned a young nobleman who had been excommunicated by the church. According to Hildegard, he repented before his death and therefore deserved, and at her instigation got, a Christian funeral and burial in consecrated ground. However, his excommunication had never been rescinded by the papal office, and in a sense, Hildegard herself revoked it. This high-handedness outraged papal authorities, who charged her with open rebellion and disobedience. As punishment, the elderly Hildegard and her community of nuns were excommunicated, a punishment that forbade them from receiving Holy Communion, from having a Christian burial, and from the use of liturgical music in their services. This censure, terrible for a medieval Christian, was removed only a few months before Hildegard's death in 1179 at the age of eighty-one.

Hildegard's genius was towering. She was the first woman to receive permission from a pope to write theological works. She was a prolific poet and author. She was a brilliant composer, the only musician of her era known both by name and by a large body of surviving musical scores. Her scientific works of natural history became standard medical texts. Her vast correspondence with popes, emperors, monarchs, and religious leaders are today monumental historical manuscripts of the Middle Ages. After her death Hildegard's countless friends and admirers recommended her for sainthood and many called her "Saint Hildegard." The church granted her only the title of "blessed."

Scivias

On Hildegard's Call

Arise therefore, cry out and tell what is shown to you by the strong power of God's help.[12]

Words of John

"For this reason the Son of God appeared, that He might destroy the works of the Devil" [1 John 3:8]. What does this mean? The great brightness, the Son of God, appeared for the health and salvation of humanity, taking on the poverty of a human body. But shining like a burning star amid shadowy clouds, He was placed on the winepress, where wine was to be pressed out without the dregs of fermentation, because He, the cornerstone, fell upon the press and made such wine that it gave forth the greatest odor of sweetness. He, shining as a glorious human being amid the human

race, without any admixture of polluted blood, trod
with His warlike foot upon the head of the ancient
serpent; He destroyed all the darts of his iniquity, full
of rage and lust as they were, and made him utterly
contemptible. Therefore whoever has knowledge in the
Holy Spirit and wings of faith, let this one not ignore
my admonition, but taste it, embrace it and receive it in
his soul.[13]

On Conquering Anger and Pride

When anger tries to burn up my tabernacle, I will look
to the goodness of God, Whom anger never touched; and
thus I will be sweeter than the air, which in its gentleness
moistens the earth, and have spiritual joy because
virtues are beginning to show themselves in me. And
thus I will feel God's goodness.

And when hatred tries to darken me, I will look to
the mercy and the martyrdom of the Son of God, and
so restrain my flesh, and in faithful memory receive the
sweet fragrance of roses that spring from thorns. And so
I will acknowledge my Redeemer.

And when pride tries to build in me a tower of vanity
without foundation on the rock, and to erect in me the
loftiness that wants no one to be like itself but always to
be taller than the rest—oh, who will help me then, when
the ancient serpent who fell into death by wishing to be
above everyone is trying to cast me down? Then I say
with grief, "Where is my King and my God? What good
can I do without God? None." But then I look to God
Who gave me life, and I run to the Most Blessed Virgin
who trod underfoot the pride of the ancient abyss, and
thus I am made a strong stone of God's edifice; and the
rapacious wolf, who choked on the divine hook, from

now on cannot conquer me. And this in God's sublimity I know the sweetest good, which is humility, and feel the sweetness of the unfailing balsam and rejoice in the delightfulness of God as if I were amid the fragrance of all perfumes. And thus I ward off the other vices by the impregnable shield of humility.[14]

The Power of God

This blazing fire that you see symbolizes the Omnipotent and Living God, who in His most glorious serenity was never darkened by any iniquity. He is *incomprehensible* because He cannot be divided by any division, or known as He is by any part of His creature's knowledge; inextinguishable because He is that fullness that no limit ever touched; wholly living, for there is nothing that is hidden from Him or that He does not know; and wholly life for everything that lives takes its life from Him. . . .[15]

The Love of God

"By this, the charity of God has appeared toward us: that God has sent His only-begotten Son into the world that we may live by Him" [1 John 4:9]. What does this mean? That because God loved us, another salvation arose than that we had in the beginning, when we were heirs of innocence and holiness; for the Supernatural Father showed His charity in our dangers, though we deserved punishment, in sending by supernal power His Holy Word alone into the darkness of the world for the people's sake. There the Word perfected all good things, and by His gentleness brought back to life those who had been cast out because of their unclean sins and could not return to their lost holiness. . . . Hence this salvation and charity did not spring from us, and we were ignorant and incapable of loving God for our salvation; but He Himself, the Creator and Lord of all, so loved His people that for their salvation He sent His Son . . . who washed and dried our wounds.[16]

God's Work in Sanctification

I had a green field in My power. Did I give it to you, O human, that you might make it put forth whatever fruit you wished? And if you sow sand in it, can you make it grow into fruit? No. For you do not give the dew, or send forth the rain, or confer fresh moisture, or draw warmth out of the burning sun, all of which are necessary to produce good fruit. So, too, you can sow a word in human ears, but into his heart, which is My field, you cannot pour the dew of compunction, or the rain of tears, or the moisture of devotion, or the warmth of the Holy Spirit, through all of which the fruit of holiness must grow.[17]

God's Help in Despair

And if the blackest tempests of blasphemy and despair fall on anyone, and he does not consent to them in his heart or his will or any perverted taste but struggles against them in great torment; then if he perseveres in the fight and strongly resists, I [God] will quickly help him. And let him not doubt because he must struggle. For I say he is a strong warrior against the greatest of storms, and I will help him most speedily and hold him as a friend; for, patiently enduring, he has nobly conquered great misfortune for love of Me.[18]

The Church Victorious

As Goliath rose up despising David, so the Devil
rose up presuming upon himself and wanting to be
like the Most High. And as Goliath was unaware of
David's strength and despised him as nothing, so the
Devil's towering pride despised the humility of the Son
of God's humanity when He was born into the world
and sought not His own glory but in all things the glory
of the Father. How? The Devil did not seek to imitate
this example and submit himself to his Creator as
the Son of God submitted Himself to His Father. But
David, with the secret strength given to him by God,
cut off Goliath's head as is written by the inspiration
of the Holy Spirit. . . . This is to say: My Son took the
spoils and booty of the Devil with His great power and
deprived the ancient serpent of his head. . . . So now
He lets the battle continue among the tents, which
are the bodies of His chosen. . . . And, to extend the
metaphor, as the glory of Goliath was given to David,
so the glory that was taken from the first angel [Satan]
was given by Me to Adam and his race, which confesses
me and keeps my precepts after the Devil's pride was
destroyed.[19]

The Mercy of God

And as a fountain should not be concealed but in
plain sight so that everyone who thirsts may come to
it and draw water and drink, so too the Son of God is
not obstructed or hidden from the elect, but is in plain
sight, preparing to requite all deeds and to show by just
rewards which ones are done for the sake of His will.
Therefore let the faithful walk to God in his faith and to
seek His mercy, and it will be given.[20]

The Use of a Good Intellect

Your Creator . . . loves you exceedingly, for you are His creature. And He gives us the best of treasures, a vivid intelligence. He commands you in the words of His law to profit from the intellect in good works and grow rich in virtue, that He, the Good Giver, may thereby be clearly known. Hence you must think every hour about how to make so great a gift useful to others as to yourself by works of justice, so that it will reflect the splendor of sanctity from you, and people will be inspired by your good example to praise and honor God. . . . And He Himself, in the sweetness of His love, will give you grace to overflowing; He will make you burn yet more for love of Him, so that, strengthened by the Holy Spirit, you may wisely discern the good and do greater deeds, and ardently glorify your Father, Who gave you these things.[21]

5

MECHTHILD

INDEPENDENT REBEL

Magdeburg, Germany; 1207–1282

Most people have had the temptation to give up when an obstacle in life seemed overwhelming. Yet one of the glories of human nature is that even in what Saint John of the Cross called "the dark night of the soul," men and women often show extraordinary fortitude. Milton captured this heroism when he wrote, "What, though the field be lost? All is not lost . . . the unconquerable will, and courage never to submit and yield . . . and what is else, not to be overcome."[1]

I have often been heartened in my own struggles by stories of women who prevailed over tremendous odds. As a child, I loved the biographies of women in history who refused to give in to their difficult circumstances. I remember sitting on our front porch during the long summer holidays reading hour by hour as the sunlight moved across the hot geraniums and ivy that spilled out of our window boxes. In my memory I am reading a biography of Mary, Queen of Scots. Later I discovered Elizabeth I of England, Catherine the Great of Russia, Joan of Arc. Eventually I came upon modern women whose lives were heroic more because of what they overcame than the grand roles history demanded of them. Helen Keller: Blind and deaf from early childhood, she became a famous author, lecturer, and humanitarian. Harriet Tubman: An escaped slave who had developed epilepsy from a blow to the head by a plantation overseer, she dedicated her life to tirelessly rescuing other slaves. Dorthea Lange: An American photographer, she traveled the world photographing the poor and oppressed but walked with a limp from childhood polio.

Mechthild of Magdeburg was a thirteenth-century German mystic who was born into wealth and ease and who chose for herself a life of tremendous hardship. Her parents were most probably members of the nobility. She was educated and cultured and had a future of great privilege. A foreshadowing of her rejection of the life that was her birthright came at the age of twelve when she had an extraordinary encounter with God. Of the vision she wrote, "And I saw with the eyes of my soul in heavenly bliss, the beautiful humanity of our Lord Jesus Christ and I knew Him by His shining countenance. I saw the Holy Trinity, the Eternity of the Father, the work of the Son and the sweetness of the Holy Spirit."[2] By the time Mechthild was a young woman of twenty-three, she had made the dramatic decision to forsake the luxury and safety of her home and her beloved family for a life of exile and extreme poverty in the city of Magdeburg, where she was unknown. Here she would devote her life to loving and serving Christ, but not as a nun. In that momentous decision she suddenly became a woman alone, unprotected, and without worldly resources.

In Magdeburg she took on the difficult life of a humble Beguine. The Beguines had arisen as a spontaneous lay-women's movement in the late twelfth century. Becoming a Beguine offered a way of life for adult women outside of the traditional roles of wife or nun. Beguines considered themselves set apart as Christ's disciples, but they did not take irrevocable life vows and did not renounce the possibility of future marriage. They often lived together in common housing, but some chose to live alone or even at home. Although the Beguines were not under the authority of any religious order, they had their own informal practices. They remained unmarried and devoted themselves to good works, especially caring for the sick and poor. They wore robes similar to those of nuns so that people would recognize them. Their three main principles were frugality, virginity, and self-knowledge.[3] Beguines looked to the early church and to Scripture in an attempt to live as much like the early apostles as possible. They were evangelists in that their chief concern was the redemption of souls. In contrast to the church, they taught that the soul's salvation was the responsibility of the individual person; heaven could not be attained by the rote following of the rites and requirements of Roman Catholicism.

A factor in the development of the Beguine movement was a widespread social predicament. In the twelfth century there was a surplus of women without husbands. Thousands of wives had been widowed by the Crusades in the East and by wars in their own countries between pope and emperor. Countless unmarried young women found themselves without prospective partners. This lack of men created a dilemma: Women were expected to live their lives under male authority and protection, either that of a father or husband within the home or of a priest within a convent. Beguines resisted the narrowness of these patriarchal options. Many did not wish to lose their independence by marrying. Others with no prospects were put in an impossible situation if they refused the cloistered and submissive life of a nun. Others were turned away from convents because their fathers could not afford the dowry of money and land that novices brought to convents for their lifelong support. Becoming a Beguine was a solution and opened up creative self-reliant alternatives for many women.

Ultimately, the Roman Catholic Church took a dim view of the Beguines. In spite of the fact that they appeared to live holy lives and gave unceasing service to the poor, they were, in the eyes of the church, unpredictable women whose lives were unsupervised by men. They further offended because they rejected the obscure Latin of the church and advocated the use of the language of the people for Bible reading and preaching. Even their lives of open simplicity and poverty were seen as devious indictments against the pomp and corruption of the clergy. By the end of the thirteenth century, Beguines became easy targets for the Inquisition and there was active persecution against them.[4] As early as 1312, the Council of Vienna had decreed that their way of life was to be permanently forbidden. The decree stated, "Since these women promise no obedience to anyone, and do not renounce their property or profess an approved Rule, they are certainly not 'religious' though they wear a habit and are associated with such religious orders as they find congenial."[5] In Mechthild's time, Beguines were marginally accepted. They dutifully made confession to priests or monks and faithfully attended mass. They had a sisterly appreciation for the orders of humble Franciscan and Dominican monks who were also committed to poverty. Like the Beguines, these monks spent their lives in caring for the poor and sick. For twenty years Mechthild struggled to serve the poor in the city of Magdeburg, but the life of a Beguine was very difficult for her. Like the apostle Paul, she found that unswerving ministry and love for Christ, even heavenly visions, did not tame one's inward nature and did not liberate one from the body.[6] "Sighing, weeping, confessing, fasting, watching, meditating, praying, these I must constantly practice."[7] Mechthild had periods of deep depression. Eventually her health failed and she was often ill. Finally she confided her deepest conflicts, longings, and experiences of God to her friend, a Dominican monk, Heinrich of Halle. Heinrich urged her to preserve in writing her insights, her spiritual battles, and her beautiful way of describing the love of her soul for Christ. Thus began the task that was to take most of the rest of her life and which produced her one book, *The Flowing Light of the Godhead.*

Mechthild began by writing on loose sheets of paper as inspiration struck her. True to Beguine principles, she wrote in Low German, the language of the people. Heinrich collected the pages of her manuscript, and eventually he organized the material into book form, possibly assisted by Mechthild. Parts of her book were circulated during her lifetime and reached a wide audience of common people who would not have been able to read them if she (or Heinrich while transcribing) had written in the Latin of the church. Although her work had many admirers, many powerful clerical critics arose. Her style of writing took many different and nontheological forms. She wrote parables, poems, dialogues, reflections, lyrics, allegories, and prayers. The dominant theme throughout her writing was that of Christ as the beloved, following the images in the Song of Songs of Scripture and the genre of courtly love literature of the troubadours.[8] She described the soul's union with God in ardent and tender language. As well, parts of her writing contained sharp criticisms of corrupt clergy. In one passage she imagines the holy church's crown: "[The crown] is dimmed in the filth of evil desires . . . the purity is burned up in the consuming fire of greed; the humility is sunk in the swamp of the flesh. . . . Alas for the fallen crown of the priesthood! . . . [God's] vengeance will come upon thee. . . . For thus saith the Lord . . . 'My sheep from Jerusalem have become wolves and murderers: for before my eyes they slay the white lambs.'"[9]

Inevitably the clerical backlash against Mechthild was fierce. There were threats to have her book burned. When she was in her early sixties, infirm, and by this time nearly blind, she was so harassed by ecclesiastical officials that she sought refuge in a Cistercian convent in Helfta, which was known for its intellectual and spiritual rigor. There, learning was greatly valued and nuns were urged to be diligent in their studies.[10] The convent was also close to the monastery that sheltered her friend, Heinrich of Halle. It was in the cloistered peace of Helfta that Mechthild wrote the final chapter to her book, and she died there in 1282.

Out of a life stalked by illness and slander, intense spiritual struggles, and unending hard work of caring for the poor, Mechthild produced writings centered on Christ as lover. Memorably, she described the soul's journey to the court of God. God sits in the heavenly palace; Christ appears as a heavenly nobleman who gives the soul her heavenly garments. Christ speaks to her in courtly language, a lovely allegory from the aristocratic traditions of medieval Germany. Today Mechthild, the ill and struggling Beguine of Magdeburg, is recognized as one of Germany's most outspoken and famous visionaries, a woman characterized by the intensity of her love for Christ and her unflagging determination to live a holy life independent of worldly and ecclesiastical privilege.

The Flowing Light of the Godhead

[A Prologue by an Unknown Writer]

This book was revealed in German by God to a sister who was a holy maiden both in body and in spirit. She served God devoutly in humble simplicity, in unheard-of poverty, and in heavenly contemplation, burdened with scorn, for more than forty years; she followed firmly and completely the light and teaching of the Order of Preachers and advanced and improved herself daily. But a brother of the same order gathered together and copied this book. Much good is in this book on many things, as is seen in the table of its contents. You should read it nine times, faithfully, humbly, and devoutly.[11]

What Hinders Spirituality

What hinders spiritual people most of all from complete perfection is that they pay so little attention to small sins. I tell you in truth: when I hold back a smile which would harm no one, or have a sourness in my heart which I tell to no one, or feel some impatience with my own pain, then my soul becomes so dark and my senses so dull and my heart so cold that I must weep greatly and lament pitiably and yearn greatly and humbly confess my lack of virtue . . . for only then I can receive the blessing of being allowed to crawl back to the kitchen like a beaten dog.[12]

Duties of a Prior

Thou shalt keep the sick cleanly, and be merry with them in a godly manner. Thou shalt also go into the kitchen and see that the needs of the brethren are well cared for, and that thy parsimony, and the cook's laziness, rob not our Lord of the sweet song of the choir, for never did starving priests sing well. Moreover, a hungry man can do no deep study, and thus must God, through such default, lose the best prayers.[13]

Prayer

It makes a sour heart sweet, a sad heart merry, a poor heart rich, a dull heart wise, a timid heart bold, a weak heart strong, a blind heart seeing, a cold heart burning. It draws the great God down to the small heart, it drives the hungry soul out to the full God, it brings together the two lovers, God and the soul, into a blissful place where they speak much of love.[14]

A Holy Dialog

Lord, I bring You my treasure. It is larger than the mountains, broader than the world, deeper than the sea, higher than the clouds, more lovely than the sun, more manifold than the stars; it weighs more than the whole earth.

O you image of My godhead, made splendid with My humanity, adorned with My Holy Spirit—What is your treasure called?

Lord, it is called my heart's desire. I have withdrawn it from the world, preserved it in myself and denied it to all creatures. But I can bear it no further. Lord, where shall I lay it?

You shall lay your heart's desire nowhere but in My divine heart and on My human breast. There alone will you be comforted and kissed by My Spirit.[15]

A Vision of Heaven

In the first choir is happiness,
the highest of all gifts,
in the second choir is meekness,
in the third choir is love,
in the fourth sweetness,
in the fifth joyfulness,
in the sixth noble tranquillity,
in the seventh riches,
in the eighth worthiness,
in the ninth burning love,
and in the sweet beyond is pure holiness . . .[16]

Praise of God

In poverty, contempt, misery, days of sorrow, spiritual poverty (that most of all) in the demands of obedience, in all kinds of bitterness, inward and outward, one can and will rejoice in praising God from the heart, thanking him with joy, reaching out to him in longing and fulfilling his will in works.[17]

A Last Word

Dear friend of God! I have written down this, my way of love, for thee. May God give it to thee in thy heart. Amen.[18]

6

MARGUERITE PORETE

"HERETIC" MARTYR

France, ∂. 1310

One of the most unforgettable people I ever met is a Russian poet called Irina Ratushinskaya. She grew up in Odessa, then capital of the Ukraine, a republic of the USSR. Her parents were descendants of Polish gentry who conformed to life in communist Russia. In spite of the model Soviet education Irina received, she rejected atheism to embrace the Orthodox Christian faith of her grandparents. In 1979 she married human rights activist Igor Gerashenko and moved with him to Kiev. In 1981 the young couple took part in a demonstration in support of Andrei Sakharov, the Russian nuclear physicist and winner of the Nobel

Peace Prize, who opposed the Soviet invasion of Afghanistan. For protesting his house arrest they were detained in Moscow and Irina spent ten days in a Butyrki prison. After her release, she lost her job as a teacher. The next year Irina was again arrested, this time for "anti-Soviet agitation and propaganda" in her poetry. For the crime of "the manufacture and dissemination of her poems," she was sentenced to seven years of hard labor in a prison camp and five years of internal exile. This judicial decision gave her the dubious distinction of receiving the longest sentence given to a woman for political crimes since the terrifying days of Joseph Stalin.

Irina was sent to a strict-regime camp called the "women's political zone" in a large women's criminal camp in Mordovia. During her imprisonment she continued to write poetry, scratching the words on soap until they were memorized and then washed away. These prison poems number more than two hundred.

In 1985 she spent six months in an isolation cell. Her head was shaved and she was fed a diet of bread and water. Between December 1983 and February 1984, in the dead of a Russian winter, she spent thirty-nine days in the worst form of isolation: an unheated punishment cell where she contracted pneumonia. Of this experience she wrote:

> I will live and survive and be asked:
> How they slammed my head against a trestle,
> How I had to freeze at nights,
> How my hair started to turn grey . . .
> But I'll smile. And will crack some joke
> And brush away the encroaching shadow.[1]

As it turned out, only four years of her brutal sentence had to be served. Release came in October 1986, on the eve of the U.S.-Soviet summit in Reykjavik, Iceland, between

President Ronald Reagan and president of the USSR, Mikhail Gorbachev.

One of the taunts her jailers made to her in her icy punishment cell was, "If you survive, you will never bear a child!" Of this, in the poem "It's Not That I'm Scared," she wrote:

It's not that I'm scared,
Just a little uneasy.
It hurts that I might not bear a son,
As the heart is giving out, and the hands grow weaker—
I try to hold on . . .[2]

After her release, in frail health, Irina came to the United States where she received the Religious Freedom Award. She spent two years as Poet in Residence at Northwestern University, Evanston, Illinois, from 1987 to 1989. She and her husband then moved to England in 1990.

I called on Irina and Igor when they were living in London in the early '90s. She welcomed me with bread and caviar along with strong coffee as we discussed Russia and poetry and the novel she was writing. The visit was transformed and distracted by the miraculous [her word] presence of her golden-haired, robust twin baby sons, watching our visit with grave interest.

Marguerite Porete, a Frenchwoman of the late thirteenth and early fourteenth centuries, resembles Irina in her indomitable will and courage. Threatened by the authorities with arrest for her writings, Marguerite remained resolute if not defiant. In due course she was arrested for heresy and went on trial before the French Inquisition. Unlike Irina, for Marguerite there was no escape from her sentence. She was burned at the stake in Paris in 1310.

Born in Hannonia, south of Flanders, Marguerite was the child of aristocratic parents and was given an excellent education, including the study of theology. As time went on, she became increasingly aware of the call of God on her life. The obvious course of action would have been to enter a convent, but she was not attracted to the nuns' vow of total, lifelong obedience to Rome. Instead she joined the Beguines.[3] By this time the Beguines were the targets of growing hostility on the part of the church, which viewed them as rivals to ecclesiastical supremacy. Particularly disconcerting to the church was the idea that sacred authority rested less on ordination and more on poverty, purity, and evangelism,[4] the very defining characteristics of the Beguines. Like other women mystics, Marguerite claimed authority for her teaching on the basis of her female weakness: Since one must give alms to the poorest being, then she, being frailty itself, was given God's word because of her neediness.

Sometime between 1296 and 1306, when she may have been around forty years of age, she composed *Mirror of Simple Souls,* written in Old French. After completing the work, Marguerite spent her time journeying from city to village, preaching and reading from her book. The audacity of an uncloistered woman setting herself up as a traveling preacher brought her to the attention of church authorities and to the theology faculty of the Sorbonne in Paris. More anticlerical than most Beguines, Marguerite saw the established church as the "Holy Church the little," which one day would give way to the invisible "greater church," which was made up of free and simple souls guided by divine love. She scandalized the bishops by writing that when a soul attains certain degrees of spiritual progress closest to God, it does not need masses, penance, sermons, fasts, or prayer. Marguerite's claim that the soul could attain a state in which it no longer needed the church or acts of penance and virtue was judged to be gravely heretical.

Marguerite wrote in the tradition of courtly love, in the form of a dialog between the Soul and Lady Reason and Lady Love. Today her teachings could be seen to approach Martin Luther's jubilant cry of "faith alone!" which sparked the Protestant Reformation some two hundred years later.

In 1306 Marguerite was brought before Guy II, the bishop of Cambrai, who condemned her book and teachings as heretical. Nothing if not dramatic, he collected all the copies of her book he could find and burned the books in front of her. She was prohibited from any future writing and from ever speaking again of her "dangerous doctrines," on pain of excommunication. Typically, Marguerite ignored her bishop's injunction. She continued to spread her ideas among the religious and the laity throughout France, even sending her book to prominent churchmen. In 1308 a new bishop, Philip de Marigny, who was also the provincial official of the Inquisition, arrested her and brought her before the court of the Inquisition on charges of leading people astray from the true teachings of Mother Church. She infuriated the local officials by refusing to answer questions or even to take the oath to tell the truth. De Marigny sent her to Paris, charged with violating the order to cease teaching and distributing her book. She remained in prison for eighteen months, maintaining her defiance. In spite of the testimony of four eminent churchmen who eloquently defended her, the Dominican Inquisitor, Master William of Paris, declared her a heretic and ordered her put to death. She was handed over to the secular French authorities for burning on the Place de Greve in Paris. She died on the stake on June 1, 1310, before an audience of people weeping because of her great learning and goodness.

In 1312 the church took formal action against the whole Beguine movement. Beguines were declared counterfeit, people having only the appearance of sanctity. They "offended the eyes of the Divine Majesty and constituted a grave danger to souls. They were a detestable sect committing execrable errors." An edict of a church council strictly forbade anyone to hold, approve, or defend the errors of the Beguines. In spite of the deadly efforts of the Inquisition, Marguerite Porete's book survived in numerous monastery copies and translations. The astonishing number of manuscripts testifies to the international popularity of her book, especially by the fifteenth century.[5] It has been read throughout the centuries as an admirable text by "an unknown French mystic."

The Mirror of Simple Souls

You who will read this book, If you want to understand
    it well
Think about what you will say,
For it is difficult to understand;
You must assume Humility, Who is the treasure of
    Science
And the mother of the other virtues,
Theologians and other clerics,
You will not have any understanding of it,
So learned are your minds,
If you do not proceed humbly
And Love and Faith together,
The mistresses of the house,
Do not cause you to surmount Reason.
Reason herself witnesses to us
In the thirteenth chapter of this book,
And is not ashamed
That love and faith give her life
And she cannot free herself from them,
For they have dominion over her,

That is why she must humble herself.
Humble, therefore, your sciences
Which are founded in Reason,
And place all your trust
In those which are given
By Love and illuminated Faith.
And thus you will understand this book
Which through Love gives life to the Soul.[6]

Seven States of the Pious Soul Which Are Otherwise Called Beings

The First State

The Soul: I have promised, says the Soul, since Love took hold, to say something about the seven states that we call beings, for this they are. They are the degrees by which one climbs up from the valley to the summit of the mountain, which is so isolated that one sees only God there; and each degree is rounded by its being. The first state, or degree, is that of the Soul touched by God through grace and stripped of her capacity to sin, who intends to keep upon her life, that is upon pain of death, the commandments God gives in the Law. And because of this Soul beholds with great fear that God has commanded her to love Him with all her heart, and her neighbor as herself, as well. To this Soul it seems labor enough for her—all that she can do—and it seems that though she love a thousand years, it is enough for her strength to hold and keep the commandments.

The Free Soul: I was once found at this point and in this state, says the Free Soul. No one is frightened to climb the heights, certainly not if she has a valiant heart full of noble courage. But the little heart from lack of love dares neither to undertake a great thing nor to climb high. Such people are cowards; this is not astonishing, for they remain in sloth which prevents them from seeking God, Whom they will never find if they do not seek Him diligently.[7]

The Second State

The second state or degree is that the Soul beholds what God advises to His special friends, beyond what He commands; he who can dispense with accomplishing all that he knows pleases his friend is no friend. And then the creature abandons herself and attempts to go beyond the advice of men by the mortification of nature, by scorning riches, delights, and honors in order to accomplish the perfection of the Gospel's counsel, of which Jesus Christ is the example. Then she fears neither losing what she has, nor the words of men, nor the weakness of the body, for her friend did not fear these things nor can the Soul who has been taken by Him.[8]

The Third State

The third state is that the Soul beholds herself affected by the love of works of perfection, works which her spirit, out of love's burning desire, decides to multiply within herself. And this makes known the subtlety of the understanding of her love, which can give no gift to her friend to comfort him except what he loves. For no other gift has any value in love than to give a friend the most loved thing. Therefore the will of this creature loves nothing except works of goodness, steadfastly undertaking all great labors with which it can nourish its spirit. For it rightly seems to her that she loves nothing

except words of goodness and thus does not know
what to give Love, unless she makes this sacrifice for
him. For no death would be Martyrdom for her except
abstaining from the work she loves, which is the delight
of her pleasure and the life of her will, which feeds on
it. Therefore she abandons these works which delight
her so and puts the will which led such a life to death,
and forces herself, the sake of martyrdom to obey the
will of others, to abstain from her work and her will,
to fulfill the will of others in order to destroy her own
will. And this is harder, very much harder than the two
aforementioned states, for it is harder to overcome
the works of the will of the spirit than it is either to
overcome the will of the body or to do the will of the
spirit. Thus one must, by breaking and crushing, reduce
oneself to powder in order to enlarge the place where
Love will want to be and must burden oneself with
several beings in order to disburden oneself and attain
one's being.[9]

The Fourth State

The fourth state is that the Soul is drawn up by
highness of love through meditation into delight of
thought, and abandons all outward labors and obedience
to others for the highness of contemplation. Then the
Soul is so difficult, noble, and delightful that she cannot
suffer anything to touch her, except the touch of Love's
pure delight which makes her singularly charming and
gay, which makes her proud of an abundance of love.
Then she is mistress of the radiance, that is to say the
light of her soul, which causes her to be marvelously
filled with love of great faith through the concord of
unions which put her in possession of her delights. Now

the soul holds that there is no higher life than to have this of which she has lordship, for Love has so fully sated her with her delights that she does not believe that God has a greater gift to give her soul here below than this love that Love has diffused in her out of love.[10]

The Fifth State

The fifth state is that the Soul beholds that God is what is, that of Whom all things are, and she is not, so she is not of that of whom all things are. And these two considerations provoke in her a marvelous astonishment and she sees that He is all goodness who has put a free will in her who is not, but is all wickedness. Now the Divine Goodness put a free will in her out of pure Divine goodness. . . . And therefore the divine Goodness diffuses before this will a ravishing diffusion of the movement of divine light. Now this Soul is seated at the very bottom, there where there is no bottom and it is low; and this lowness causes her to see very clearly the true Sun of highest goodness, for she has nothing which keeps her from this sight. And this divine Goodness shows Himself to her out of goodness that draws her upward and transforms her and unites her body by a bond of goodness with pure divine Goodness.[11]

The Sixth State

The sixth state is that the Soul neither sees herself, whatever the abyss of humility she may have within herself, nor God, whatever high goodness He may have. But God sees Himself in her through His divine majesty that illuminates this Soul of Himself, so that she sees that no one is but God Himself Who is that of Whom all things are; and what is God Himself. And therefore she sees but herself; for who sees what is sees only God Himself, Who, through His divine majesty, sees Himself in the Soul herself. And then the Soul in the sixth state is freed from all things and pure and illuminated—but not glorified, for the glorification is in the seventh state, that we will have in glory about which no one can speak. But this Soul, thus pure and illuminated, sees neither God nor herself but rather God sees Himself by Himself in her, for her, Who (that is to say God) shows her that there is nothing except Himself. And for this reason the soul knows nothing except Him, and thus loves but Him and praises but Him, for there is nothing except Him.[12]

The Seventh State

The Seventh State keeps Love within the Soul to give us everlasting glory, which we will not know until our soul has left our body.[13]

7

JULIAN

LOVING HERMIT

Norwich, England; 1343–ca. 1416

I grew up in a foster home in Ontario, Canada, experiencing a childhood that was shaped by long-held English parenting adages. One was that children should be seen and not heard. My foster parents owned a neighborhood grocery store, and they had little spare time for a child underfoot. "Go read a book!" was the invariable remedy for childish chatter, boredom, worry, curiosity, fretfulness, fatigue. An inexhaustible supply of materials was required for this book system of child management. Thus, I was introduced at a tender age to the public library. I recall being much taken with the high windows, the sun streaming in like a yellow river, and the faint papery smell of books. The shoelaces of my sturdy oxfords were often untied, and when I stooped to clumsily retie them, I liked the shiny brown

5

2

linoleum covering the floor, and how it was worn down at the librarian's checkout counter.

Another strictly held maxim in my foster home was that to praise a child or to express affection would disastrously spoil a child. I have since observed that this idea is not exclusive to the English. As unlike the English as Russians are, they have a widely-held version of this adage, convinced that it is bad luck for parents to compliment their own children. Cautious parents inevitably refer to their offspring in disparaging ways in order to ward off the evil eye. My foster parents would have been scandalized by the idea of an evil eye, but they would have agreed with the general sentiment.

History and literature are replete with examples of English children from various classes who were reared without the daily praise and affection of their parents. Biographies of Winston Churchill describe how as a small boarding-school boy he wrote pleading letters to his mother begging her to visit him and to let him come home during school holidays. In Charles Dickens's era, poor children had to be sent by their parents to work alone long hours in factories. Among the upper classes, legions of Mary Poppinses relieved mothers of the presence of and responsibility for their offspring.

I wouldn't entirely recommend the English system of child-rearing as a method of creating warmly expressive adults. People brought up in the cool and ordered climate of an English childhood can ever after be slightly daunted by expansive expressions of affection. Certainly reserve and "a stiff upper lip" seem to be national and often admirable characteristics of the English. Yet it is an English-woman, Julian of Norwich, greatest and most beloved of the English visionaries, who gave the world a lavish and beautiful interpretation of the unwavering love of God.

Julian's visions of the flowing and measureless love of the Godhead were so powerful that she reflected on them for the rest of her life. Her holy optimism today "stands unexcelled for its compassion and its psychological acuity."[1]

Julian was born in the eastern English city of Norwich in 1343 in a catastrophic time. The Black Death was sweeping across the European continent. By the time Julian was five years old, the plague had crossed the English Channel into Britain. Before it subsided, one third of the population had died. Panicked people by the thousands fled infested cities to the countryside in the hope of escaping death. Others fatalistically held debauched orgies while awaiting their end. Many flocked to the churches to plead for mercy; belief that the plague was a punishment from God was widespread. Even churches left without priests were crowded with penitents trying to appease God's wrath.[2]

With so many dying, there came to be a critical shortage of labor throughout the country. Few were left to plant and harvest, to tend to the livestock, to nurse the sick, to preach the sermons, to care for the children. Bitter quarrels broke out between desperate religious orders, peasants were hungry and rebellious, and early reformers, repelled by the excesses and abuses of the church, cried out for change. Followers of John Wycliffe, called Lollards, precursors of Protestantism, were increasingly hunted down, some burned alive in pits less than a mile from Norwich. The tragic Hundred Years' War between France and England was waged throughout Julian's lifetime and a further catastrophe, the Great Schism of the Western Church, took place in 1378 following the death of Pope Gregory XI. To the end of her days both the pope in France and the pope in Rome claimed to be the true vicar of Christ and bitterly condemned the other as the Antichrist.

Fear and foreboding hung over the whole of England as the prevailing context of Julian's life.

Her birthplace of Norwich was a busy town of considerable importance, although its population had been decimated by the plague. Norwich had three colleges for priests and a great Norman cathedral with an impressive library. Outside of the city was a community of Benedictine nuns who ran a school for well-born young girls. There, it is believed, Julian was educated in Scripture, Latin, rhetoric, and secular writings. As a young woman she was deeply devout. She wrote that in these years she asked three graces from God. The first was that she would be enabled to live her life in the remembrance of Christ crucified. The second was that she would experience bodily sickness when she was thirty, the same age as Jesus when he began his ministry. The last grace that she requested was that she would have three "wounds": true repentance, loving compassion, and a constant longing for God.

In her thirtieth year, Julian indeed became gravely ill. Her condition was so critical that on Easter morning, May 6, 1373, she was given the Last Rites of the Church in anticipation of her death. All feeling was gone from her waist down, and her sight had begun to fail. Two days later it appeared that her death was imminent, and the parish curate was sent for. He came carrying a crucifix so that the cross of Christ could be the last object she saw in this life. But Julian did not die. Instead, for the next eleven hours she received a series of sixteen visions of Christ. When the revelations stopped, her full recovery was almost immediate. Julian quickly wrote down in the Middle English of her day an account of these visions called *Revelations of Divine Love*.

Following this remarkable experience, Julian decided to give her life wholeheartedly to meditation and prayer.

She became an anchorite, a person called to solitude who was confined alone until death. Anchorites lived in small, unfurnished rooms built onto the outside walls of cathedrals or churches. Their cells had three windows: one opening into the church so that mass could be heard and the Sacrament received, one to communicate with a servant, and one to hear the questions and troubles of people who came to her for counsel. Julian's room was attached to a corner of the modest parish church of Saint Julian of Norwich, from which she is given the name "Julian." She lived in that space for the rest of her life. Saint Julian's was just off one of the main streets of Norwich, and Julian's window was easily accessible to the increasing numbers of people who came to her for advice and comfort.

After twenty years of contemplation and prayer, Julian felt God's call to expand the writing of her early account of her "deathbed" visions. This she did in a second and longer version of *Revelations*. Her writing brought immeasurable comfort to an anxious people still gripped by the fear of death and the fear of God's anger. To all who came to her or read her writing, Julian serenely repeated Christ's words to her that "All will be well, all will be well, and all manner of things will be well." To those tormented by their sins and the dread of hell, she said that God's eternal purpose was not to condemn and punish the world, but to bring all people into the bliss of heaven.

Julian had a strong and unusual sense of Christ as mother. She compared his ministry to that of a human mother who suckles her child with her own milk. Jesus as mother intimately feeds his children with himself by means of his body and blood. Christ is not *like* a mother: He is as *really* mother as he is father and all the tenderness that motherhood implies are found in Christ's care for his own. The relationship between a mother and her child was to Julian the closest comparison humans can make to the relationship between Jesus and the soul. Very little else is known about Julian. She was not a nun, and at some time she became known as "Mother" [Dame] Julian. It is thought she died around the year 1416.

Revelations of Divine Love

Rest

For this is the cause why we be not all in ease of heart and soul: that we seek here rest in those things that are so little, wherein there is no rest, and know not our God that is All-mighty, All-wise, All-good. For He is the Very Rest. God willeth to be known, and it pleaseth Him that we rest in Him; for all that is beneath Him sufficeth not us. And this is the cause why that no soul is rested till it is made nought as to all things that are made. When it is willingly made nought, for love, to have Him that is all, then it is able to receive spiritual rest. Also our Lord God shewed that it is full great pleasance to Him that a helpless soul come to Him simply and plainly and homely.[3]

Feelings

. . . It is speedful to some souls to feel on this wise: sometimes to be in comfort and sometimes to fail and be left to themselves. God willeth that we know that He keepeth us even alike secure in woe and in weal [happiness]. And for profit of man's soul, a man is sometimes left to himself . . . But freely our Lord giveth when He will; and suffereth us [to be] in woe sometime. And both is one love.[4]

All Will Be Well

After this the Lord brought to my mind the longing that I had to Him afore. And I saw that nothing letted [hindered] me but sin. And so I looked, generally, upon us all, and methought: *If sin had not been, we should all have been clean and like our Lord, as He made us.*

And thus, in my folly, afore this time often I wondered why by the great foreseeing wisdom of God the beginning of sin was not letted: for then, methought, all should have been well. This stirring [of mind] was much to be forsaken, but nevertheless mourning and sorrow I made therefor, without reason and discretion.

But Jesus . . . answered by this word and said : *It behoved [was necessary] that there should be sin; but all shall be well, and all shall be well, and all manner of things shall be well.* [5]

Assurance

And thus our good Lord answered to all the questions and doubts that I might make, saying full comfortably: I may make all thing[s] well, I can make all things well, I will make all things well, and I shall make all things well; and thou shalt see thyself that all manner of thing will be well. . . . And in these five words God willeth we be enclosed in rest and in peace. [6]

Worry

. . . I desired to learn assuredly as to a certain creature that I loved, if it [sic] should continue in good living, which I hoped by the grace of God was begun. And in this desire for a *singular* Shewing, it seemed that I hindered myself: for I was not taught in this time. And then was I answered in my reason, as if it were by a friendly intervenor: *Take it GENERALLY, and behold the graciousness of the Lord God as He sheweth to thee: for it is more worship [glory] to God to behold Him in all than in any special thing.* And therewith I learned that it is more worship to God to know all-thing[s] in general, than to take pleasure in any special thing. And if I should do wisely according to this teaching, I should not only be glad for nothing in special, but I should not be greatly distressed . . . for ALL shall be well. For the fulness of joy is to behold God in all.[7]

Prayer

Full glad and merry is our Lord of our prayer; and He looketh thereafter [from then on] and He willeth to have it because with His grace He maketh us like to Himself in condition as we are in kind [while we are still in our natural conditions]: and so is His blissful will. Therefore, He sayeth thus: *Pray inwardly, though thee thinketh it savour [pleases] thee not, though thou feel not, though thou see nought; yea, though thou thinkest thou canst not. For in dryness and in barrenness, in sickness and in feebleness, then is thy prayer well-pleasant to me, though thou thinkest it savour thee nought but little.*[8]

Trust

For this is our Lord's will, that our prayer and our trust be both alike large. For if we trust not as much as we pray, we do not full worship to our Lord in our prayer, and also we tarry [torment, tire] and pain our self. The cause is, as I believe, that we know not truly that our Lord is [the] Ground on whom our prayer springeth; and also that we know not that it is given us by the grace of His love. For if we knew this, it would make us to trust to have, of our Lord's gift, all that we desire.[9]

Peace

. . . God is our very Peace, and He is our sure Keeper when we are ourselves in unpeace, and He continually worketh to bring us into endless peace. And thus when we, by the working of mercy and grace, be made meek and mild, we are fully safe; suddenly is the soul oned [united] to God when it is truly peaced in itself: for in Him is found no wrath. And thus I saw that when we are all in peace and in love we find no contrariness . . . For that contrariness is the cause of our tribulations and all our woe, and our Lord Jesus taketh them and sendeth them up to Heaven, and there are they made more sweet and delectable than heart may think or tongue may tell. And when we come thither [to heaven] we shall them ready, all turned into very fair and endless worships.[10]

Failure

. . . He suffereth some of us to fall more hard and more grievously than ever we did afore, as us thinketh. And then ween [consider] we (who be not all wise) that all were nought that we have begun. But this is not so. For it needeth us to fall, and it needeth us to see it. For if we never fell, we should not know how feeble and how wretched we are of our self, and also we should not fully know that marvelous love of our Maker. For we shall see verily in heaven, without end, that we have grievously sinned in this life, and notwithstanding this, we shall see that we were never hurt [less precious] in His love, we were never the less price in His sight. And by the assay [trial] of this falling we shall have an high, marvelous knowing of love in God without end. For strong and marvelous is that love which may not, nor will not be broken for our trespass.[11]

God's Mothering

But oftentimes when our falling and our wretchedness is shewed us, we are so sore adread, and so greatly ashamed of our self, that scarcely we find where we may hold us [hardly know what to do]. But then willeth not our courteous Mother that we flee away, for Him were nothing other [nothing could be further from what He wants]. But He willeth then that we use the condition of a child: for when it is hurt or adread, it runneth hastily to the mother for help, with all its might. So willeth He that we do, as a meek child saying thus: *My kind Mother, my Gracious Mother, my dearworthy Mother, have mercy on me: I have made myself foul and unlike to Thee, and I nor may amend it but with thine help and grace.* And if we feel us not then eased forthwith, be we sure that He useth the condition of a wise mother. For if He see that be more profit to us to mourn and to weep, He suffereth [allows] it with rue [compassion] and pity until the best time, for love. And He willeth then that we use the property of a child, that evermore of nature trusteth to the love of the mother in weal or in woe.[12]

Depression

. . . And [when] we fall again to our heaviness, and spiritual blindness, and feeling of pains spiritual and bodily, by our frailty, it is God's will that we know that He hath not forgotten us. And so signifieth He in these words: *And thou shalt never more have pain; no manner of sickness, no manner of misliking, no wanting of will; but ever joy and bliss without end.*

It is God's will that we take His behests [promises] and His comfortings as largely and as mightily as we may take them, and also He willeth that we take our abiding and our troubles as lightly as we may take them, and set them at nought. For the more lightly we take them, and the less price we set on them, for love, the less pain we shall have in the feeling of them, and the more thanks and meed [reward] we shall have of them.[13]

Self-Worth

And then our Lord opened my spiritual eye and shewed me my soul in midst of my heart. I saw the Soul so large as it were an endless world, and as it were a blissful kingdom. And . . . I understood that the soul is a worshipful [glorious] City. In the midst of that City sitteth our Lord Jesus, God and Man . . . most majestic King, most worshipful Lord; and I saw Him clad majestically . . . And the Godhead ruleth and sustaineth heaven and earth and all that is [but] the place that Jesus taketh [is] in our Soul. He shall never remove it, without end, as to my sight: for in us is his homliest [inviting, cozy] home and his endless dwelling.[14]

Confidence

He said not: *"Thou shalt not be tempted, thou shalt not be tempested, thou shalt not be travailed [distressed]";* but He said, *"Thou shalt not be overcome."*[15]

Reverence

Flee we to our Lord and we shall be comforted, touch we Him and we shall be made clean, cleave we to Him and we shall be sure and safe from all manner of evil. For our courteous Lord wills that we should be as homely [close] to Him as heart may think or soul may desire. But [let us] beware that we take not so recklessly this homeliness as to leave [neglect] courtesy . . . and if we wot [know] not how we shall do all this, desire we of our Lord and He shall teach us; for it is His own good pleasure and His worship [glory]; blessed may He be![16]

God's Perspective

If any such lover [Christian] be in earth which is continually kept from falling, I know it not: for it was not shewed me. But this was shewed: that in falling and in rising we are ever preciously kept in one Love. For in the Beholding [sight] of God we fall not, and in the beholding of self we stand not; and both these [manners of beholding] be sooth [truth] to my sight. But the Beholding of our Lord God is the highest soothness. Then are we greatly bound to God [for] that He willeth in this living to shew us this high soothness . . . For the higher Beholding keepeth us in spiritual solace and true enjoying in God . . . unto the time that we be brought up above, where we shall have our Lord Jesus unto our meed [reward] and be fulfilled of joy and bliss without end.[17]

CATHERINE

Siena, Italy; 1347–1380

I had a friend in grade school named Jenny Harmansky. Her parents were immigrants from the Ukraine who came to Canada to work in the steel company factory by Hamilton Bay. I was in awe of Jenny and her family because they were so unlike the lower-middle-class English society of my foster parents. Jenny looked different. She had long frizzy hair that her mother braided into one thick braid hanging down her back and tied at the end with a gauzy white ribbon. Nobody's mother did that. Jenny lived next door and I was sometimes, reluctantly, in her house. It smelled funny. It had linoleum on all the floors, even in the living room. Large framed photographs hung so high up on the walls you couldn't really see them, and her mother couldn't speak

English. Her unwavering silence made me think that she knew dark and important secrets, and I feared her.

One day Jenny and I were walking along the street together and I described a picture in my aunt's Bible. It was a panorama of judgment with sinners twisting in hell and good people wafted heavenward by angels. Jenny was appalled. "Never, never read the Bible," she whispered in alarm. *"My mother* says people go crazy when they read the Bible." I felt a horrible chill. Was it too late for me? I had looked at the words too. Jenny thought I would be all right. People had to shut themselves up in a room and read the Bible all day and *then* they would go crazy.

I can imagine Mrs. Harmansky's grim diagnosis of people who saw visions. She would have had a simple explanation for the complex and intense Catherine of Siena whose spiritual journey began at age six with a powerful vision.

From all accounts, Catherine was an enchanting little girl. In her very early childhood, reports describe her as a child so captivating that her many relatives and family friends constantly invited her to their homes on some pretext or other so they could enjoy her childish gaiety. This early playfulness was to end only too soon. One day Catherine was walking along a hilly country road with one of her brothers. Suddenly she saw a vision of Christ, surrounded by angels and saints. The vision so profoundly affected her that from that time on she devoted her small self to prayer, meditation, and spiritual disciplines. Her parents, busy working-class people who lived in Siena, probably paid little attention to Catherine's pious "play." She was, after all, their twenty-third child.

Undeterred by Catherine's unusual piety, her mother began looking around for a husband for her when the girl was in her early teens. Catherine resolutely refused to consider any suitors on the grounds that she belonged only to God and had dedicated her virginity to Christ when she was seven. Her mother ignored her protestations. Catherine then cut off all her hair so that suitors might be discouraged by her scandalous appearance. Her mother, enraged at her behavior, dismissed the servants and made Catherine do the heavy household work. Catherine accepted the punishment sweetly and worked hard, while continuing her religious disciplines of sleeping on boards and fasting. Her weight fell dramatically. Her worried and exasperated mother took the young teen to a health spa. Catherine sought out the scalding source of the hot springs in order to suffer burns. She also managed to contract an illness, thought to be a mild case of smallpox, which further marred her appearance. Around this time her father became convinced of her religious vocation; he allowed Catherine to have a small room to herself in the family home and ordered the household not to interfere with her.

Catherine longed to join a Dominican "third" order as a Sister of Penance. As a third-order sister, she would not be a cloistered nun, but would live at home, free to give herself over to spiritual disciplines. The Sisters of Penance were older widows and were somewhat alarmed at the prospect of this unusual young girl joining them, but eventually they agreed. Catherine spent the next three years of her life shut away in a small room in her father's house, meditating, fasting, and praying, leaving her room only to walk to mass. In the early part of her seclusion she suffered excruciating demonic torments, which, after extended suffering, brought her into a profound and highly personal communion with Christ.

When she was nineteen, her life changed again. Christ told her to end her solitude and go out among people to do for them what she couldn't do for him. She immediately entered back into the daily life of her large and extended family, taking on the arduous tasks of her family's household. The family must have been startled by her appearance. The three years of fasting had taken its inevitable toll. She was no longer the hearty teenager she had been, having lost almost half her body weight. In spite of her weakened physical condition, she worked tirelessly and with good cheer. As a Sister of Penance not in seclusion, she was expected to nurse the sick. Obediently, Catherine made her way to the hospital of Santa Maria Della Scala and discovered she had a natural talent for nursing. Never one to do anything by halves, she chose as her patients the worst cases, those who were the sickest and most disfigured with leprosy and terminal cancer. In the course of caring for the sick she communicated such a deep devotion to them and a gift of healing that growing numbers of people, sick and well, sought her out. Her aristocratic sister-in-law began to accompany her in her daily hospital rounds to shield her from the crowds who flocked to her for advice and counsel. Even families in the midst of fiery blood feuds that had passed on from generation to generation fell on their knees in her presence and were reconciled. Loyal friends and followers gathered around her, listening to her teaching and assisting her in practical ways.

Her severe fasting continued during these years and at around the age of twenty-five, it is said that she stopped eating altogether and slept less than an hour in every twenty-four. Her failure to eat is well attested by both friends and by skeptics who would have disproved it if they had been able.[1] Her circles of influence continued to widen as admiration for her holiness of life and her spiritual wisdom grew.

When she was twenty-seven she was called to Florence for an interview with the Master-General of the Dominican order. He was so impressed by her spiritual gifts and by those who had gathered around her as her spiritual family, he assigned a Dominican superior, Raymond Capus, to her and her following. Capus became her personal confessor, lifelong friend, and a chronicler of her life.

As Catherine's world expanded, she became painfully aware of the terrible times in which she lived. The plague had returned to Italy, decimating the population. The Holy Roman Church was in bitter disarray. Pope Clement V lived in ease in France. Rome, former cradle of the church, was in turmoil. The moral state of the clergy was, according to Catherine herself, one of deepest degradation, and she began to exert a tremendous effort toward reform. She persuaded priests who were living in luxury to give away their possessions and to live simply.

In Catherine's time, the papal office still had supreme authority over the church throughout the Western European kingdoms. Earlier, in the twelfth and thirteenth centuries, the prestige of the papacy had been so great that popes attempted to dominate the emperors and kings of Europe. These efforts met with tremendous opposition as secular armies clashed with armies loyal to the pope. In Italy, the papal states had descended into turmoil and anarchy. In 1309 Pope Clement V had abandoned Rome for the pastoral safety of Avignon, France. The seat of the Bishop of Rome, founded on the tombs of Saints Peter and Paul for more than a thousand years, was now empty. From then on, the papacy fell under the control of the French kings, and subsequent popes were French, elected by the French-dominated College of Cardinals. The authority of these French popes was not accepted in all countries of Europe, and certainly not in Italy, and thus Latin Christendom was deeply divided.

Catherine was passionately convinced that the present French pope, Gregory XI, had to return to his rightful
place in Rome in order to unify the fragmented church
and to draw back to Rome the wealth and power of the
papacy. She was twenty-nine when she undertook an arduous journey from Italy to France to the magnificent papal
palace in Avignon. She was received by Pope Gregory XI,
who listened to her pleas that he return to Rome and initi-
ate reform of the clergy. Pope Gregory was so impressed
by Catherine's diplomatic gifts that he appointed her his
delegate to the rebellious Italian city-state of Florence,
which had risen in revolt against the Avignon regime. In
December of 1376 Catherine succeeded in negotiating a
tenuous peace between Florence and the pope. To her great
joy, in January of the New Year of 1377, Gregory returned
the papacy to Rome in spite of the furious opposition of
France and the French cardinals.

The last five years of Catherine's life, from 1375 to 1380,
were spent as diplomat, teacher, and writer. She went again
to Florence in her attempts to bring a second reconciliation
between the papacy and the rulers of the Florentine state.
She undertook a preaching crusade at Pisa and tried to
influence the city to support Gregory. About this time she
felt called to begin writing. For several months she stayed
outside Siena secluded at a castle where she began writing
the *Dialog*. Her book took the form of four conversational
essays between Divine Providence and the human soul
(represented by Catherine), on discretion, prayer, providence, and obedience. The keynote to Catherine's teaching
is that a person, whether in the cloister or in the world,
must ever abide in the cell of self-knowledge in which the
traveler through time to eternity must be born again.[2]

Pope Gregory's death in 1378 brought confusion and
disarray to the church. The cardinals elected an Italian

pope, Urban VI, who to Catherine's dismay turned out to be tyrannical and corrupt. Catherine worked tirelessly to persuade Urban to mend his ways, and she loyally attempted to induce the church to accept him as the true pope. The cardinals asserted that his election had been invalid and elected a new pope, Clement VII, who ruled from Avignon. Undaunted, Catherine rebuked both sides. To three cardinals who supported the French pope she wrote, "What made you do this? You are flowers who shed no perfume, but a stench that makes the whole world reek."[3] She wrote to the Italian pope, rebuking him for pride and arrogance.

Urban invited Catherine to his palace in Rome, where she spent the last two years of her life in exhausting struggles to assist Urban in his attempts to reorganize the church. From Rome she tirelessly dictated letters and exhortations in attempts to gain support for the Italian pope, thus hoping to unify Western Christendom. Frail and exhausted, Catherine, reclining on boards, died in 1380 at the age of thirty-three, her goal of a united church unreached.

Catherine's holiness of life, wisdom, and reforming influence was so remarkable that she was canonized by Pope Pius II in 1461. Six hundred years after her death she was made a doctor of the church[4] by Pope Paul VI in 1970, an honor that recognizes Catherine's unprecedented initiative, reforming zeal, and spiritual wisdom. She is the first of only two female doctors in Roman church history, taking her place with the great Teresa of Avila and a company of medieval scholars and saints, including Augustine, Aquinas, and Francis of Assisi. She said of herself, "Fire is my nature." The metaphor is apt. Her life was like a meteor that streaked across the sky of fourteenth-century Europe: dramatic, powerful, and quickly gone. What has been left to posterity are her incomparable writings, all of which had to be dictated, which include almost four hundred letters, twenty-six prayers, and the four treatises which make up her timeless book.

The Dialog of Catherine of Siena

A Treatise of Divine Providence

How a soul, elevated by desire of the honor of God, and of the salvation of her neighbours, exercising herself in humble prayer, after she had seen the union of the soul, through love, with God, asked of God four requests.

The soul, who is lifted by a very great and yearning desire for the honor of God, and the salvation of souls, begins by exercising herself, for a certain space of time, in the ordinary virtues, remaining in the cell of self-knowledge, in order to know better the goodness of God toward her. This she does because knowledge must precede love, and only when she has attained love, can she strive to follow and to clothe herself with the truth.

. . . So that soul, wishing to know and to follow the truth more manfully, and lifting her desires first for herself—for she considered that a soul could not be of use, whether in doctrine, example or prayer, to her neighbor, if she did not first profit herself, that is she did not acquire virtue in herself—addressed four requests to the Supreme and Eternal Father. The first was for herself, the second for the reformation of the Holy Church; the third a general prayer for the whole world, and in particular for the peace of Christians who rebel, with much lewdness and persecution against the Holy Church; in the fourth and last, she besought the Divine Providence to provide things in general, and in particular, for a certain case with which she was concerned.[5]

A Treatise of Discretion

*How the affection should not place reliance chiefly
on penance, but rather on virtues; and how discretion[6]
receives life from humility . . .*

[Jesus speaks to Catherine in a vision.] "These are the
holy and sweet works which I seek from My servants;
these are the proved intrinsic virtues of the soul, as I
have told thou. They not only consist of those virtues
which are done by means of the body, that is, with
an exterior act, or with diverse and varied penances
which are the instruments of virtue; works of penance
performed alone without the above-mentioned virtues
would please Me little; often, indeed, if the soul performs
not her penance with discretion, that is to say, if her
affection be placed principally in the penance she has
undertaken, her perfection will be impeded; she should
rather place reliance on the affection of love, with a
holy hatred of herself, accompanied by true humility
and perfect patience . . . with hunger and desire for My
honour and the salvation of souls. . . . That is, [the soul]
should place her principal affection in virtue rather
than penance. Penance should be but the means to
increase virtue according to the needs of the individual
and according to what the soul sees she can do in the
measure of her own possibility.

". . . This virtue of discretion is no other than a true
knowledge which the soul should have of herself and of
Me, and in this knowledge is virtue rooted . . . that which
gives life to the tree, to its branches and its root is the
ground of humility . . . humility is the foster-mother and
nurse of charity by whose means this tree remains in the
perpetual calm of discretion.

"And I have already said to you, that the root
of discretion is a real knowledge of self and of My

goodness, by which the soul immediately . . . [renders] praise and glory to My Name, and in referring to Me the graces and the gifts which she sees and knows she has received from Me . . .

". . . For when [people] have rendered what is due to Me and to themselves, they proceed to render to their neighbor their principal debt of love, and of humble and continuous prayer, which all should pay to each other and further, an example of a holy and honorable life, counseling and helping others according to their needs for salvation."[7]

A Treatise of Prayer

Of the means which the soul takes to arrive at pure and generous love; and here begins the Treatise of Prayer.

[Christ speaks] When the soul has passed through the doctrine of Christ crucified, with true love of virtue and hatred of vice and has arrived at the house of self-knowledge and entered therein, she remains, with her door barred, in watching and constant prayer, separated entirely from the consolations of the world. Why does she shut herself in? She does so from fear, knowing her own imperfections, and also from the desire, which she has, of arriving at pure and generous love. And because she sees and knows well that in no other way can she arrive thereat, she waits, with a lively faith for My arrival, through increase of grace in her. How is a lively faith to be recognized? By perseverance in virtue and by the fact that the soul never turns back for anything, whatever it be, nor rises from holy prayer, for any reason except (note well) for obedience or charity's sake. For no other reason ought she to leave off prayer, for, during the time ordained for prayer, the Devil is wont to arrive in the soul, causing much more conflict and trouble than when the soul is not occupied in prayer. This he does in order that holy prayer may become tedious to the soul, tempting her often with these words, *"This prayer avails thee nothing, for thou needest to attend to nothing except thy vocal prayers."* He acts thus in order that, becoming wearied and confused in mind, she may abandon the exercise of prayer, which is a weapon with which the soul can defend herself from every adversary, if grasped by the hand of love, by the arm of free choice in the light of the Holy Faith.[8]

A Treatise of Obedience

Here begins the treatise of obedience, and first of where obedience may be found, and what it is that destroys it, what is the sign of a man's possessing it, and what accompanies and nourishes obedience.

The Supreme and Eternal Father, kindly turning the eye of His mercy and clemency toward her, replied, ". . . Thou wilt find [obedience] in its completeness in the sweet and amorous Word, my only-begotten Son. So prompt in Him was this virtue that in order to fulfill it, He hastened to the shameful death of the Cross. What destroys obedience? Look at the first man, and you will see the cause. . . . It was pride, which was produced by self-love, and desire to please his companion. This was the cause that deprived him of the perfection of obedience, giving him instead disobedience, depriving him of the life of grace, and slaying his innocence, therefore he fell into impurity and great misery, and not only him but the whole human race . . . The sign that thou hast this virtue is patience and impatience the sign that you have it not, and you will find that this is indeed so. . . . Since I saw that man whom I so much loved, did not return to Me, his End, [I] took the keys of obedience and put them in the hands of my sweet and amorous Word - the - Truth - and He became the porter of that door, opened it, and no one can enter except by that door and that Porter.

What caused the great obedience of the Word? The love which he had for My honour and your salvation. Whence proceeded this love? From the clear vision with which His soul saw deeply into God and the eternal Trinity. . . . And inasmuch as love cannot be alone, but is accompanied by all the true and royal virtues, because all the virtues draw their life from love, He possessed them all . . . patience, which is the marrow of obedience, and a demonstrative sign, whether a soul be in a state of grace and truly love or not. Wherefore charity, the mother of patience, had given her as a sister to obedience and so closely united them together that one cannot be lost without the other. . . . This humility is the foster-mother and nurse of charity, with the same milk she feeds the virtue of obedience. Her raiment given to her by this nurse is self-contempt and insult, desire to displease herself, and to please Me. Where does the soul find this? In sweet Christ Jesus, My only-begotten Son. For who abased himself more than He did? He was sated with insults, jibes, and mockings. He caused pain to Himself . . . to please Me. And who was more patient than He? For His cry was never heard in murmuring, but He patiently embraced His injuries . . . Wherefore in Him thou wilt find obedience perfectly accomplished. . . . He is the way, wherefore He said, *"He was the Way, the Truth and the Life."* For he who travels by that way travels in the light and . . . cannot stumble or be caused to fall, without perceiving it.[9]

TERESA

REFORMER AND VISIONARY

Avila, Spain; 1515–1582

Teresa of Avila was a Spanish mystic of the sixteenth century with brilliant spiritual gifts, one of which was her tremendous zeal for organization and reform. Reformers in the heat of their passion are often both admired and feared, as was Teresa. They are loved only in retrospect. I have found this true in my one and daunting experience with a tireless reformer, my diminutive and aged high school Latin teacher, Miss Snell. Miss Snell had an abhorrence of idleness that would have made her and Teresa kindred souls. In her small and required Latin class, we students aspired to learn only enough Latin to pass the final exam at the end of the year, which was a grade of 50 out of an impossible 100. Miss Snell's reformation took the form of an unflagging campaign in her classroom against laziness and indifference. Her means were Roman in the swiftness and rigor of her discipline. Errors were punished. Unfinished homework was doubled. Inattention, the worst misdeed, earned a dreaded command to stand and immediately translate a new passage from the Latin. Both Miss Snell in her classroom at Delta Collegiate and Teresa in her convent at Avila wanted nothing less than hearts humbled and changed. Teresa was enlivened by the love of God; Miss Snell, by the glory that was Rome.

In addition to the Latin language, Miss Snell taught us Roman virtues. She loved the Roman genius for organization and order and the virtues of *gravitas,* responsibility; *pietas,* devotion to family and country; and *justitia,* the sense of what is naturally right. She sometimes read us virtue-laden English translations from the Latin poets or Shakespeare's *Julius Caesar.* Early on we memorized Livy's words on Horatio holding the Sublican Bridge against the Etruscan army:

> Then out spake brave Horatius
> The Captain of the Gate:
> "To every man upon this earth
> Death comes soon or late;
> And how can man die better
> Than facing fearful odds,
> For the ashes of his fathers
> And the temples of his gods?"

The aim of this exercise actually was to identify the English words in the given passage that came from Latin roots. So insistent was she that not one word be missed that to this day I find myself obsessively alert to English words originating in Latin, as if Miss Snell might suddenly materialize and demand to know if I were paying attention. Translating the occasional Latin phrase one might come upon in ordinary reading has become a serious obligation. Sometimes on a Sunday morning, when our church choir sings a Latin anthem at the offertory, I try to translate as they go along, and when I check the English words in the bulletin for help, I do so furtively.

From our beginning in her first form class until we passed the matriculation examination four years later, Miss Snell tirelessly preached discipline as the all-purpose remedy for weariness, difficulty, lack of time, and the common social distractions of high school. Discipline was the royal and only road to both learning and virtue. In this I fondly think she was not far from wrong. Discipline, however, was probably a practice that had small part in the childhood of Teresa of Avila, which makes her adult life all the more interesting and surprising.

Teresa was born in 1515 into a prosperous mercantile family during Spain's golden age. The Italian Christopher Columbus had moved to Spain and having received the sponsorship of Isabella I and Ferdinand V of Castile had sailed to America in 1492. The opening of the New World made Spain one of the richest and most powerful countries in Europe. New ideas were flourishing everywhere. When Teresa was two years old, far to the north in Germany, Martin Luther nailed his ninety-five theses to the church door in Wittenberg to call for sweeping reform in the Catholic Church. Spanish Avila, however, was a sleepy and contented place, the dark granite wall encircling the city seemingly protecting its Catholic community from the winds of change. Teresa's father followed the tradition of the Spanish upper class and saw to it that Teresa was taught to read and write and that she learned the womanly arts of sewing and spinning in preparation for her future role as a patrician Spanish matron and mother.

There is reason to believe that as a little girl Teresa had a lively religious imagination and persuasive powers. When she was a young child, determined to die for Christ, Teresa convinced her older brother Rodrigo to set off with her to Islamic lands where they could become Christian martyrs at the hands of the infidel Muslims. The children managed to reach a nearby town before an uncle found them and returned them home to their parents, who would most certainly not have been amused. Later on, she and Rodrigo wrote a book on chivalry, the knightly code of behavior that included religious piety, social graces, and combat for glory and Christian purposes. This was a highly unusual achievement for children and it consequently attracted a great deal of attention. As Teresa entered adolescence, she is said to have been beautiful, with dark curly hair, large expressive eyes, and graceful hands. She loved pretty clothes and perfumes and had a personal charm that was irrepressible and winsome. She greatly enjoyed the social life of Avila and her lively spirit and sense of humor brought her many friends.

When Teresa was fourteen, her mother died, and Teresa helped her father with her siblings. By the time she was sixteen, a romance of sorts began with a neighbor boy that was serious enough that Teresa's father and brothers might have had to be called upon to defend her honor.[1] Teresa was sent away to a strict Augustinian convent school where she stayed for almost two years. To her surprise, she realized that she was happy in the convent, even though she did not want to become a nun. Her other option was marriage, which she dreaded, having seen her mother, Dona Beatriz, grow weak from multiple pregnancies (her first when Dona Beatriz was barely thirteen),[2] ultimately to die in giving birth to her ninth child at the age of thirty-three.

112

After Teresa's return from the convent school, she continued to help her father raise her younger brothers and sisters and to enjoy much popularity in the town. In the motherless household where Teresa coped daily with her rowdy siblings, she gradually lost her reluctance to consider a vocation as a nun. Her father had other plans: He wanted her to marry. In 1535 when she was twenty, she defied her father's wishes and secretly entered the Carmelite Convent of the Incarnation at Avila. It is said that as Teresa was hurriedly leaving her home for the convent, a man appreciatively gazed at her ankles as she climbed into her carriage. "Take a good look," she called out to him, "that's the last one you'll get!"[3] Eventually her disappointed father relented and gave the convent Teresa's ample dowry. Teresa took her vows a year later as Sister Teresa of Jesus.

Teresa had been a nun less than two years when she became gravely ill and was sent to stay with her half-sister, Dona Maria. Her condition may have been a form of catalepsy, a strange deathlike disorder in which a person falls into a trancelike state. The body position or facial expression does not change, and the arms and legs of the person remain in any position in which they are placed. Today catalepsy is associated with narcolepsy, epilepsy, and occasionally hysteria. Eventually Teresa returned to her convent, weak and unable to move, and the effects of the paralysis remained until the summer of 1542, when she was twenty-seven. Further episodes of the illness continued to recur for at least a decade, and for the rest of her life her health remained frail.

For her first twenty long years as a nun, Teresa endured intense spiritual struggles. When she was ill, she tried to concentrate on her prayer life but she experienced devastating spiritual dryness. In the times when she was well, she indulged in the easy social life of her convent, where her high spirits and amusing wit were much in demand. Many women of the aristocracy had entered the Carmelite order, donating their lavish dowries to the community. The nuns lived in comfortable apartments of their own inside the convent, had servants, ate well, and could freely entertain friends and have as many visitors and interests as they liked. They were even allowed to move back and forth from the convent to the town for extended visits and for dinners and parties. Teresa found herself enjoying a worldly life with many admirers among the sisters and townspeople. Yet she was tormented by guilt.

> It is one of the most painful lives, I think, that one can imagine; for neither did I enjoy God nor did I find happiness in the world. When I was experiencing the enjoyments of the world, I felt sorrow when I recalled what I owed to God. When I was with God, my attachments to the world disturbed me. This is a war so troublesome that I don't know how I was able to suffer it even a month, much less for so many years.[4]

When she was thirty-nine, Teresa began to experience a deep religious awakening after, as she said, "nearly twenty years on that stormy sea [of spiritual despair]." She read *The Confessions of St. Augustine,* identifying with Augustine's illnesses and his long struggle to free himself from pride and sensuality. Teresa found greater peace in prayer and a sense of joy and love that extended into her daily life. Visions of "the sorely wounded Christ" came to her and she sensed interior voices that brought her comfort and counsel. Painfully aware of both her past sins and the vigilant Spanish Inquisition that sought out heretics, she turned to spiritual confessors to help her discern if her visions were from God. In these interviews, Teresa was so convincing about her unworthiness that some of the clergy concluded that her visions had to be the work of Satan. Of her precarious situation she wrote, "Without doubt I fear those who have such great fear of the devil more than I do the devil himself."[5] Other clergy believed that her visions were authentic. Word quickly spread about the ambiguous case of this well-known nun so that the whole city of Avila was alive with speculations. In time, through the intervention of a number of godly Dominican and Jesuit fathers, her visions were validated.

Teresa had found a new freedom and happiness in her spiritual life, but her distress about the worldly life of her convent grew. By the year 1567, at the age of fifty-one, she was passionately convinced that the careless discipline of the Carmelites must be reformed. Originally, the order had been founded in the twelfth century by hermits on Mount Carmel in Palestine as a contemplative religious order devoted to prayer and poverty. Teresa looked back to the Carmelite beginnings as her model. Her order ought to be strictly confined within the convent with no communication with outsiders. The nuns' days should be spent in solitary study and prayer, and the order should be *discalced,* a word that means, literally, *shoeless,* a symbol of poverty and humility. Unsurprisingly, Teresa's sister nuns were startled, appalled, and resistant to reform.

A niece of Teresa's, also a Carmelite, eventually persuaded Teresa to found a smaller Carmelite house of her own, which kept more closely to the original intentions of the order. When Teresa's aspirations to build a new convent became known, there was a great outcry of disapproval by the nuns at the very idea that she would leave. They were joined by the local nobility, town officers, and highly offended townspeople who saw her determination to build a new convent as ambitious and prideful. Nevertheless,

Teresa began raising funds for the project. Her resolve was supported by the Bishop of Avila, and she found a generous donor in a local wealthy widow. After bitter opposition, in 1562 she succeeded in founding the Convent of Discalced Carmelite Nuns of the Primitive Rule of Saint Joseph at Avila. In due course, approval came from Rome for Saint Joseph's strict practices of worship, contemplative prayer, and poverty. Like the Augustinians of her childhood, the Saint Joseph nuns, aristocrat or wealthy women as they may have been, begged for their food and labored for their simple needs.

From this small beginning, a Catholic reform movement was ignited in Spain with Teresa as a leading figure. She had tremendous success in establishing and linking convents throughout the country. She traveled tirelessly in all weathers, braving thieves and rat-infested inns, establishing reformed convents. Teresa's organizational genius was equally practical and mystical, and she was a shrewd judge of character. She detested religious cant and people who considered themselves saints in their own opinions.

In spite of the many hardships she endured in her travels, and the opposition from church authorities that she often encountered, her wit and humor remained intact. On one occasion she was invited to found a convent by an archbishop, but when she arrived in the pouring rain, he ordered her to leave. "And the weather so delightful too" was her comment on the debacle. Once when she was tossed from a carriage, she exclaimed, "Lord, if this is how you treat Your friends, no wonder You have so few!" As she traveled, Teresa's combination of spirituality, intelligence, and repartée made many friends, most famously Saint John of the Cross, the great Spanish mystic and poet-priest, also a Carmelite. He joined Teresa in her zealous mission and with her guidance and encouragement he founded fourteen discalced monasteries for men. Because of his fervor for reform, he so angered the entrenched church hierarchy that he was imprisoned in Toledo and tortured. Teresa herself made bitter enemies in the church and she was continuously harassed by hostile church officials.[6] A papal delegation from Rome was sent to Spain to investigate her. The envoy's report to the pope was far from favorable. He described Teresa as a restless gadabout, a disobedient, stubborn, ambitious woman teaching harmful doctrine as if she were a professor.

Some of Teresa's superiors who knew of her visions and voices had long urged her to write about them for the edification of the church. At first Teresa vigorously objected to committing her spiritual experiences to writing. She produced a litany of excuses: It was for learned men to do the writing. There were more than enough books on prayer and other spiritual matters. She had neither the health nor the wits for writing. She had spinning to do. Finally, however, she gave in to the admonishments of her superiors and began to write her first book, an autobiography, *Life of Teresa*, which was composed from 1562 to 1565. Although a spiritual autobiography, it is also a treatise on prayer. *The Way of Perfection* (written after 1565) was composed to give her nuns further instructions on prayer, and *Inner Castle* (1577), perhaps her greatest work, describes the inner, spiritual stages of the contemplative life. By the time she finished writing, she had produced twelve books and hundreds of letters, all which were published after her death.

Teresa's writings have become spiritual masterpieces, known for their spontaneity and freshness, works that have gained a steady audience, widening from the sixteenth century to the present. Her writing is permeated by the love of God and characterized by her humor, intelligence, and pragmatism. She had a remarkable ability to express profound religious truths in a style that is rich in imagery and yet accessible to ordinary readers.

Despite her frail health and the resistance to reform by factions in the church hierarchy, she continued to travel and establish reformed convents until 1575. She was then sixty and teaching at a convent in Seville. There a bitter dispute broke out over which branch of the Carmelites had authority over the region. Teresa had tried to prevent such a conflict but failed. In order to defuse the situation, she was ordered to retire to a convent in Castile. Five years later, broken in health, she was released by Pope Gregory XIII, with permission to resume her reforms. This she did for the next two years until she was fatally stricken on a return journey to Avila and died at the age of sixty-seven. The Carmelite reforms that Teresa ignited in Spain flowed into the great Catholic Counter-Reformation. Her efforts purified the church in Spain and defended Spain against the Protestant Reformation that swept across much of Northern Europe. Only forty years after her death, still during the Counter-Reformation, Teresa received canonization. This honor is a declaration of sainthood and entitles the person to be fully reverenced as a saint by the Roman Catholic Church. Four hundred years after her death, in 1970, Teresa, along with Catherine of Siena, was declared a doctor of the church by Pope Paul VI.

Teresa's contemporaries saw a woman of iron determination, humility, and honor. "I just laughed at myself," she writes. She calls herself (one wonders how seriously) "incompetent and unprofitable." Her inner life with Jesus, however, as evidenced through her writing, was one of incomparable sweetness.

"Who are you?" her Beloved asked her one afternoon.

"I am Teresa of Jesus," she had murmured, "and who are you?"

"I am Jesus—of Teresa." [7]

Interior Castle

First Mansions

I began to think of the soul as if it were a castle made of a single diamond of very clear crystal, in which there are many rooms, just as in heaven there are many mansions[8]. . . . As to what good qualities there may be in our souls, or Who dwells within them, or how precious they are—those are things which we seldom consider and so we trouble little about carefully preserving the soul's beauty. All our interest is centered in the rough setting of the diamond and in the outer wall of the—that is to say, in these bodies of ours.[9] As far as I can understand, the door of entry into this castle is prayer and meditation.[10] So long as we are buried in the wretchedness of our earthly nature, these streams of ours will never disengage themselves from the swamp of cowardice, pusillanimity[11] and fear. We shall always be lancing around and saying, "Are people looking at me or not?". . . "Dare I begin such and such a task?" "Is it pride that is impelling me to do so?" "Can anyone as wretched as I engage in so lofty an exercise as prayer?" "Will people think better of me if I refrain from following the crowd?" "For extremes are not good," they say, "even in virtue."[12]

The light which comes from the palace occupied by the King hardly reaches these first mansions at all. This is not because there is anything wrong with the room, but because there are so many bad things—snakes and vipers and poisonous creatures that have come in with

the soul that they prevent it from seeing the light . . .
which force [the soul] to close [its] eyes to everything
but themselves. This seems to me to be the condition of
a soul which, though not in a bad state, is so completely
absorbed in things of the world, in possessions and
honours or business . . . and seems quite unable to free
itself from these impediments.

Everyone, however . . . will be well advised, as
far as his state of life permits, to try to put aside
all unnecessary affairs and business. . . . It is most
important that we should not cease to be watchful
against the devil's wiles, lest he deceive us. Let us realize
that true perfection consists in the love of God and of
our neighbour. . . .[13]

Second Mansions

This chapter has to do with those who have already
begun to practice prayer and who realize the importance
of not remaining in the first Mansions. . . . But it is a
very great mercy that they should contrive to escape
from the snakes and other poisonous creatures, if only
for short periods, and should realize that it is good to
flee from them. In some ways, these souls have a much
harder time than those in the first Mansions; but they
are in less peril.

These souls, then can understand the Lord when
He calls them. . . . He becomes a very good Neighbour
to them. And such are His mercy and goodness that,
even when we are engaged in our worldly pastimes
and businesses and pleasures, and haggles, when we
are falling into sins and rising from them again . . . in
spite of all that, this Lord of ours is so anxious that we
should desire Him and strive after His companionship,

that He calls us ceaselessly and this voice of His is so
sweet . . .

His appeals come through the conversation of good
people, or from sermons, or through the reading of good
books and there are many ways which you have heard in
which God calls us. Or they come through sickness and
trials . . . or in prayer. You must not . . . be disconsolate,
even though you have not responded immediately to
the Lord's call; for His Majesty is quite prepared to wait
many days, and even years, especially when He sees we
are persevering and have good desires. This is the most
necessary thing here; if we have this, we cannot fail to
gain greatly. Nevertheless, the assault which the devils
now make upon the soul, in all kinds of ways, is terrible.
. . . For here the devils once more show the soul . . .
the things of the world—and they pretend that earthly
pleasures are almost eternal: they remind the soul of
the esteem in which it is held in the world, of its friends
and relatives, of the way its health will be endangered by
penances . . . and of impediments of a thousand other
kinds. . . .

On the other hand, reason tells the soul how mistaken
it is in thinking that all these earthly things are of the
slightest value by comparison with what it is seeking;
faith instructs it in what it must do to find satisfaction;
memory shows it how these things come to an end,
and reminds it that those who have derived so much
enjoyment from the things which it has seen, have died
. . . The will inclines to love One in Whom it has seen so
many acts and signs of love . . . Then the understanding
comes forward and makes the soul realize that, for
however many years it may live, it may never hope to
have a better friend . . . It is reflections of this kind which
vanquish devils.[14]

If, then, you sometimes fall, do not lose heart, or cease striving to make progress, for even out of your fall, God will bring good. . . .[15]

Third Mansions

. . . concerning the souls that have entered the third Mansions: in enabling these souls to overcome their initial difficulties, the Lord has granted them no small favour, but a very great one. They use their time well; they practice works of charity toward their neighbours; and they are very careful in their speech and dress and in the governing of their households if they have one . . .[16] Yet do not suppose God has any need of our works; what He needs is the resoluteness of our will.[17]

I have known a few souls who . . . have for many years lived an upright and carefully ordered life, both in soul and in body, and then His Majesty has sent them tests . . . and they have become restless and depressed in spirit . . . they brood over their woes and make up their minds that they are suffering for God's sake, and thus never really understand that it is all due to their own imperfection . . . They then realize that this is a way of testing them, they gain a clear perception of their shortcomings, and sometimes they derive more pain for, finding that, in spite of themselves they are still grieving about earthly things, and not very important things, either . . . This, I think, is a great mercy on the part of God, and even though they are at fault, they gain a great deal in humility.[18]

. . . let us leave our reason and our fears in His hands and let us forget the weakness of our nature which is apt to cause us so much worry . . . our progress has nothing to do with the body, which is the thing that matters least.

What the journey . . . demands is great humility. In these present mansions the Lord does not fail to recompense us with just measure and even generously for He always gives us much more than we deserve by granting us a spiritual sweetness much greater than we can obtain from the pleasures and distractions of this life.[19]

Let us look to our own shortcomings, and leave other people's alone; for those who live carefully ordered lives are apt to be shocked at everything and we might well learn very important lessons from the persons who shock us.[20]

Fourth Mansions

As these mansions are now getting near to the place where the King dwells, they are of great beauty and there are such exquisite things to be seen and appreciated in them that the understanding is incapable of describing them . . . in order to reach these mansions, one must have lived a long time in the others . . . but there is no infallible rule about it.

[Concerning] the difference between sweetness in prayer and spiritual consolations—it seems to me that we may describe as sweetness what we get from our meditations and from petitions made to our Lord. This proceeds from our own nature, though, of course, God plays a part in the process. . . . This spiritual sweetness arises from the actual virtuous work which we perform and we think we have acquired it by our labours.

We are quite right to feel satisfaction at having worked in such a way. But when we come to think of it, the same satisfaction can be derived from numerous things that may happen to us here on earth. When for example, a person suddenly acquires some valuable property; or equally meets a person whom he dearly loves . . . It seems to me that the feelings that come to us from Divine things are as purely natural as these except that their source is nobler, although these worldly joys are in no way bad.

[Souls] would do well, however to spend short periods in making various acts, and in praising God and rejoicing in His goodness and in His being Who He is, and in desiring His honour and glory. It goes a long way toward reawakening the will. The important thing is not to think much but to love much. Love consists in the firmness of our determination to try to please God in everything and to endeavour, in all possible ways, not to offend Him.[21]

Fifth Mansions

How shall I ever be able to tell you of the riches and the treasures and the delights which are to be found in the fifth Mansions?[22] . . . That soul has now delivered itself into His hands and His great love has so completely subdued it that it neither knows nor desires anything save that God will do with it what He wills . . . the soul in that state does no more than the wax when a seal is impressed upon it—the wax does not impress itself . . . it is soft . . . it does not impress itself; it is only prepared for the impress; that is, it is soft; it merely remains quiet and consenting.[23]

I see people very diligently trying to discover what kind of prayer they are experiencing and so completely wrapped up in their prayers that they seem afraid to stir . . . I realize how little they understand of the road to the attainment of union . . . If you see a sick woman to whom you can give some help, never be affected by the fear that your devotion will suffer, but take pity on her; if she is in pain, you should feel pain too; if necessary, fast, so that she may have your food, not so much for her sake but because you know it to be your Lord's will . . . Again, if you hear someone being highly praised, be much more pleased than if they were praising you.

You must do violence to your own will so that your sister's will is done in everything, even though this may cause you to forgo your own rights and forget your own good in your concern for theirs, and however much your physical powers may rebel. If the opportunity presents itself, too, try to shoulder some trial in order to relieve your neighbor of it. Do not suppose it will cost you nothing or that you will find it all done for you. Think what the love which [Christ] had for us cost Him, when in order to redeem us from death, He died such a grievous death as the death of the Cross.[24]

Sixth Mansion

There is another way in which God awakens the soul . . . [which is] by means of His locutions[25] which are of many kinds. Unless [the speaking] agrees strictly with Scripture take no more notice of it than you would if it came from the devil himself. The words may in fact, come only from your weak imagination.

The surest signs that one can have of their coming from God are as follows: the first and truest is the sense of power and authority which they bear with them, both in themselves and in the actions which follow them. I will explain myself further. A soul is experiencing all the interior disturbances. . . . A single word . . . just a "Be not troubled"—is sufficient to calm it.

The second sign is that a great tranquillity dwells in the soul, which becomes peacefully and devoutly recollected, and ready to sing praises to God . . . The third sign is that these words do not vanish from the memory for a very long time: some indeed, never vanish at all.[26]

Seventh Mansion

. . . In this mansion everything is different. Our good God now desires to remove the scales from the eyes of the soul so that it may see and understand something of the favour which He is granting it . . . First of all the spirit becomes enkindled and is illuminated as it were by a cloud of the greatest brightness. It sees these three Persons, individually and yet by a wonderful kind of knowledge that is given to it, the soul realizes that most certainly and truly all these three Persons are one Substance and one Power and one Knowledge and one God alone . . .[27] As far as I can understand, the effects are these: First, there is a self-forgetfulness which is so complete that it really seems as though the soul no longer existed because it is such that she has neither knowledge nor remembrance that there is either heaven or life or honour for her, so entirely is she employed in seeking the honor of God.

The second effect [is] that whatever His Majesty does, she considers to be for the best: if He wills that she should suffer, well and good, if not she does not worry herself to death as she did before. There are hardly any of the periods of aridity or interior disturbance in it which at one time or another have occurred in all the rest, but the soul is almost always in tranquillity.[28]

You must not build upon foundations of prayer and contemplation alone, for unless you strive after the virtues and practice them, you will never grow to be more than dwarfs.[29] Apart from praying for people, by which you can do a great deal for them, do not try to help everybody. By your doing things that you really can do, His Majesty will know that you would like to do many more, and thus He will reward you exactly as if you had won many souls for Him.[30]

CONCLUSION

We women of faith stand today on our bit of earth, the world around us swirling with beauty and opportunity. We are blessedly free from the ecclesiastical fears and perils of our sisters of the deep Christian past. We know, even if we seldom think of it, that twenty-first-century women in the West are the most privileged women in the history of the world.

We look back at Perpetua, parting from her infant son as she walks to her death in a Roman arena. She is joined a thousand years later by Marguerite Porete, who walked to the fire. There is Dhuoda, helpless as we will never be, locked in her castle, worriedly writing spiritual directions to her doomed teenage son. We consider Egeria's years of wandering across Europe driven by her passion for biblical learning. There is Hildegard, a true genius of her age, demurely pretending to the men that she is "a mere woman and inadequate." The beautiful Catherine, fasting and faint, confronts the pope himself, calling him to holy repentance. And Julian in her small cell in Norwich assures the sick and plague-terrified that "all will be well and all manner of things will be well." Teresa, famously laughing at her own foibles and weaknesses, becomes a resolute hero of reformation in the Spanish church.

What strikes me most about these women is their strength and honor. Nothing deterred them from their deep love of Jesus and their unflagging loyalty to him. Some paid with their lives, others with their reputations and their security, relinquishing the comforts of family and the joys of motherhood. Still, they pressed on in a holy dignity. They surely represent the lives of countless women down through the ages who could not put their experiences and insights into writing, women who did not become famous but whose lives of quiet and costly discipleship would be no less inspiring if we knew of them.

But of course, we do. They are our friends, our mothers and sisters and daughters. They are the elderly women, praying in their pews. They are the young mothers sharing their faith with their children. They are the working women, denigrated as "religious," and the Christian women in helping professions who tirelessly serve the suffering.

They are ourselves, flawed and graced and loved by God. We follow in a holy and unbroken train.

NOTES

Chapter 1: Perpetua

1. A new believer in the early church under instruction in the rudiments of Christianity; a prerequisite to baptism.

2. P. Dronke, *Women Writers of the Middle Ages* (Cambridge, Mass.: Cambridge University Press, 1984), 1.

3. P. Wilson-Kastner, ed., *A Lost Tradition: Women Writers of the Early Church* (Washington, D.C.: University Press of America, 1981), 20.

4. Ibid., 21–24.

5. A common meal mainly called a "love feast," shared by early Christians as a visual expression of the love they felt for each other as cosharers of the love of Christ.

6. The "Gate of Life" through which victors left the arena.

7. Wilson-Kastner, 26–29.

8. Ibid., 30.

Chapter 2: Egeria

1. Church of the Holy Sepulcher, Jerusalem.

2. M. Thiebaux, *The Writings of Medieval Women* (New York: Garland Publishing, 1994), 23.

3. N. Davies, *Europe: A History* (Oxford: Oxford University Press, 1996), 240.

4. G. Gingras, *Egeria: Diary of a Pilgrimage* (New York: Newman Press, 1970), 8.

5. Ibid., 9.

6. J. Wilkinson, *Egeria's Travels* (London: SPCK Press, 1973), 174–75.

7. Ibid., 177–78.

8. God caused the Israelites in the wilderness to sicken and die because of their gluttony in consuming the quail he had sent them.

9. Gingras, 49.

10. Ibid., 72–74.

11. A church built over the tomb of a martyr or in honor of a martyr.

12. A distinction was made between those believers who had been prepared for baptism and those who were awaiting instruction, generally a required two-year period.

13. From 6 A.M. until 9 A.M.

14. The week before Easter Sunday.

15. A vaulted ceiling.

16. Gingras, 122–24.

Chapter 3: Dhuoda

1. K. Wilson, ed., *Medieval Women Writers* (Athens, Ga.: University of Georgia Press, 1984), 12.

2. Ibid., 13.

3. Ibid., 15.

4. Ibid.

5. Ibid.,16.

6. Ibid.

7. Ibid., 19.

8. Ibid., 20.

9. Ibid., 22.

10. Ibid., 24.

11. Ibid., 25.

Chapter 4: Hildegard

1. F. Beer, *Women and Mystical Experience in the Middle Ages* (Woodbridge, Sussex: Boydell Press, 1992), 19.

2. "Abbess," *Microsoft Encarta Encyclopedia 2000* (Microsoft Corporation, 1993–99).

3. Beer, 16.

4. M. Brady, Review of B. Newman, *Voice of the Living Light: Hildegard of Bingen and Her World* in *Northwestern Magazine,* January/February 1999, 38.

5. M. Fox, ed., *Hildegard of Bingen's Book of Divine Works: With Letters and Songs* (Sante Fe, N.M.: Bear & Company, 1987), ix–xix.

6. For an essay on medieval gardens see A. Kemp-Welch, *Of Six Medieval Women with a Note on Medieval Gardens* (Williamstown, Mass.: Corner House Publishers, 1972), 173–89.

7. C. Hart and J. Bishop, trans., *Hildegard of Bingen: Scivias.* (New York: Paulist Press, 1990), 59.

8. Beer, 30.

9. E. Pagels, *Adam, Eve, and the Serpent* (Harmondsworth, England: Penguin Books, Ltd., 1988), 63.

10. B. Newman, *Sister of Wisdom: St. Hildegard's Theology of the Feminine* (Berkeley, Calif.: University of California Press, 1987), 250.

11. Essentials of music, www.essentialsofmusic.com/composer/hildegard.html (10 October 2002).

12. Hart and Bishop, 67. Headings by Myrna Grant.

13. Ibid., 105.

14. Ibid., 115.

15. Ibid., 150.

16. Ibid., 162–63.

17. Ibid., 228.

18. Ibid., 233.

19. Ibid., 320–21.

20. Ibid., 436.

21. Ibid., 479–80.

Chapter 5: Mechthild

1. J. Milton, "Paradise Lost, Book 1" in *The Complete Poetry of John Milton*, ed. J. Shawcross (New York: Bantam Doubleday Dell, 1963), 105.

2. Beer, 80.

3. Thiebaux, 387.

4. Beer, 80.

5. C. Flinders, *Enduring Grace* (New York: HarperSanFrancisco, 1993), 50.

6. "It seems to be a fact of life that when I want to do what is right, I inevitably do what is wrong. I love God's law with all my heart. But there is another law at work within me that is at war with my mind. That law wins the fight and makes me a slave to the sin that is still within me. Oh, what a miserable person I am. Who will free me from this life that is dominated by sin?" (Rom. 7:21–24).

7. Beer, 81.

8. Thiebaux, 388.

9. Beer, 82–83.

10. Ibid., 103.

11. Ibid.,163.

12. Ibid., 168.

13. A. Kempe-Welch, *Of Six Medieval Women* (1913; reprint, Williamstown, Mass.: Corner House Publishers, 1972), 68.

14. Ibid., 68.

15. Wilson, 179.

16. Ibid., 172.

17. J. Nichols and L. Shank, *Peace Weavers: Medieval Religious Women* (Kalamazoo, Mich.: Cistercian Publications, 1987), 232.

18. A. Oden, *In Her Own Words* (Nashville: Abingdon Press, 1994), 147.

Chapter 6: Marguerite Porete

1. I. Ratushinskaya, *No, I'm Not Afraid* (Newcastle Upon Tyne, England: Bloodaxe Books, 1986), 132.
2. I. Ratushinskaya, *Pencil Letter* (New York: Alfred A. Knopf, 1989), 49.
3. See the discussion of the Beguine movement on pages 65–67.
4. Wilson, 207.
5. Ibid., 209.
6. Ibid., 210–211.
7. Ibid., 220.
8. Ibid.
9. Ibid., 221.
10. Ibid.
11. Ibid., 222.
12. Ibid., 224.
13. Ibid.

Chapter 7: Julian

1. Flinders, 101.
2. Davies, 412.
3. G. Warrack, ed., "Julian of Norwich (1373)," *Revelations of Divine Love* (London: Methuen & Company, 1901), 11.
4. Ibid., 35.
5. Ibid., 55–56.
6. Ibid., 62.
7. Ibid., 70–71.
8. Ibid., 85–86.
9. Ibid., 87–88.
10. Ibid., 104.
11. Ibid., 153.
12. Ibid., 154.
13. Ibid., 161–62.
14. Ibid., 154.
15. Ibid., 167.
16. Ibid., 189.
17. Ibid., 198.

Chapter 8: Catherine

1. Flinders, 118.
2. E. Gardener, "St. Catherine of Siena," Catholic Encyclopedia, 1908, www. newadvent.org/cathen/03447a.htm (2 October 2002).
3. "Catherine of Siena (1347–1380)," in V. Scudder, ed. and trans., *St. Catherine of Siena as Seen in Her Letters* (London: Dent, 1906), 99–100.

4. A doctor of the church is bestowed by a specific papal action and requires sanctity of life, soundness of doctrine, and canonization, that is, the person already has been declared a saint.
5. A. Thorold, trans., *The Dialogue of Catherine of Siena* (Rockford, Ill.: Tan Books & Publishers, Inc., 1907), 26–28.
6. Spiritual discernment.
7. Thorold, 50–53.
8. Ibid., 158–59.
9. Ibid., 281–84.

Chapter 9: Teresa

1. Flinders, 162.
2. Ibid., 161.
3. Ibid., 155.
4. Teresa of Avila (1565), *Autobiography*, in Flinders, 167.
5. Flinders, 157.
6. G. Alt, ed., *Teresa of Avila, Saint,* Microsoft Encarta Encyclopedia (Seattle: Microsoft Corporation, 2000).
7. Flinders, 190.
8. St. Teresa of Avila (1577). *Interior Castle,* trans. & ed., E. A. Peers. (New York: Image Books, 1961), 28.
9. Ibid., 28.
10. Ibid., 29.
11. Timidity.
12. Peers, 39.
13. Ibid., 41–42.
14. Ibid., 46–49.
15. Ibid., 51.
16. Ibid., 59.
17. Ibid., 61.
18. Ibid., 62–63.
19. Ibid., 66–67.
20. Ibid., 69.
21. Ibid., 72–76.
22. Ibid., 96.
23. Ibid., 109.
24. Ibid., 116–17.
25. Speakings.
26. Peers, 140–42.
27. Ibid., 209.
28. Ibid., 222.
29. Ibid., 229.
30. Ibid., 233.

BIBLIOGRAPHY

Alt, G. "Abbess." *Microsoft Encarta Encyclopedia*. Seattle: Microsoft Corporation, 2000.

Alt, G. "Teresa of Avila, Saint." *Microsoft Encarta Encyclopedia*. Seattle: Microsoft Corporation, 2000.

Beer, F. *Women and Mystical Experience in the Middle Ages*. Woodbridge, Sussex: Boydell Press, 1992.

Brady, M. Review of Newman, B., *Voice of the Living Light: Hildegard of Bingen and Her World. Northwestern Magazine*, January/February 1999, 36–38.

Davies, N. *Europe: A History*. Oxford: Oxford University Press, 1996.

Dronke, P. *Women Writers in the Middle Ages*. Cambridge, Mass.: Cambridge University Press, 1984.

Flinders, C. *Enduring Grace*. New York: Harper Collins, 1993.

Fox, M. ed., *Hildegard of Bingen's Book of Divine Works: With Letters and Songs*. Sante Fe, N.M.: Bear & Company, 1987.

Gardener, E. "St. Catherine of Siena." Catholic Encyclopedia (1908). www.newadvent.org/03447a.htm (2 October 2002).

Gingras, G. *Egeria: Diary of a Pilgrimage*. New York: Newman Press, 1970.

Hart, C. and J. Bishop, trans. *Hildegard of Bingen: Scivias*. New York: Paulist Press, 1990.

Kempe-Welch, A. *Of Six Medieval Women with a Note on Medieval Gardens.* Williamstown, Mass.: Corner House Publishers, 1973.

Milton, J. "Paradise Lost, Book 1." *The Complete Poetry of John Milton.* Edited by J. Shawcross. New York: Bantam Doubleday Dell, 1963.

Newman, B. *Sister of Wisdom: St. Hildegard's Theology of the Feminine.* Berkeley, Ca.: University of California Press, 1987.

Nichols, J., and L. Shank. *Distant Echoes.* Kalamazoo, Mich.: Cistercian Publications, 1984.

Oden, A. *In Her Own Words: Women's Writings in the History of Christian Thought.* Nashville: Abingdon Press, 1994.

Pagels. *Adam, Eve and the Serpent.* Harmondsworth, England: Penguin Books, 1988.

Peers, E. A., trans. *Interior Castle.* New York: Image Books, 1961.

Ratushinskaya, I. *No, I'm Not Afraid.* Newcastle Upon Tyne, England: Bloodaxe Books, 1986.

Scholer, D. *Women in Early Christianity.* New York: Garland Publishing, 1993.

Scudder, V., ed. and trans. *St. Catherine of Siena as Seen in Her Letters.* London: Dent, 1926.

Thorold, A., trans. *The Dialog of Catherine of Siena.* Rockford, Ill.: Tan Books and Publishing, 1907.

Warrack, G., ed. *Revelations of Divine Love.* London: Methuen & Company, 1901.

Wilson, K. *Medieval Women Writers.* Athens, Ga.: University of Georgia Press, 1984.

Wilson-Kastner, P., ed. *A Lost Tradition: Women Writers of the Early Church.* Washington, D.C.: University Press of America, 1981.

Myrna Grant (Ph.D., Northwestern University) is the author of several books and articles, a book reviewer, and emerita associate professor of Communications, Wheaton College. She lives in Wheaton, Illinois.